WOMEN
OF SOUTH AFRICA
Their Fight for Freedom

Women South Africa

Their Fight for Freedom

Photographs by PETER MAGUBANE

Text by Carol Lazar

Introduction by Nadine Gordimer

A BULFINCH PRESS BOOK

Little, Brown and Company

Boston ■ Toronto ■ London

First Edition

The author gratefully acknowledges Sached Trust/
Macmillan Boleswa for permission to reprint the
following poems from its publication *Voices from
Young Africa:*
"Shack Dwellers" by Mhlanganisi Ngonyama,
"Domestic Workers" by Grance Tiny Sithebe,
"I want to be free" by Julia Cumes.

The photograph of Peter Magubane on page 119 is
by Paul Belasco.

Book design: James Stockton and Associates

Library of Congress Cataloging-in-Publication Data
Magubane, Peter.
    Women of South Africa : their fight for freedom/
photographs by Peter Magubane : text by Carol
Lazar : introduction by Nadine Gordimer. — 1st ed.
        p.   cm.
    "A Bulfinch Press book."
    ISBN 0–8212–1928–6 (hc)
    ISBN 0–8212–1934–0 (pb)
    1. Apartheid — Pictorial works.   2. Women —
South Africa — Pictorial works.   3. South Africa —
History — 1961– — Pictorial works.
    I. Lazar, Carol.   II. Title.
DT1757.M35   1993
968′.00496′0082 — dc20   92-27774

Bulfinch Press is an imprint and trademark of Little,
Brown and Company (Inc.)
Published simultaneously in Canada by Little, Brown
& Company (Canada) Limited

PRINTED IN THE U.S.A.

Contents

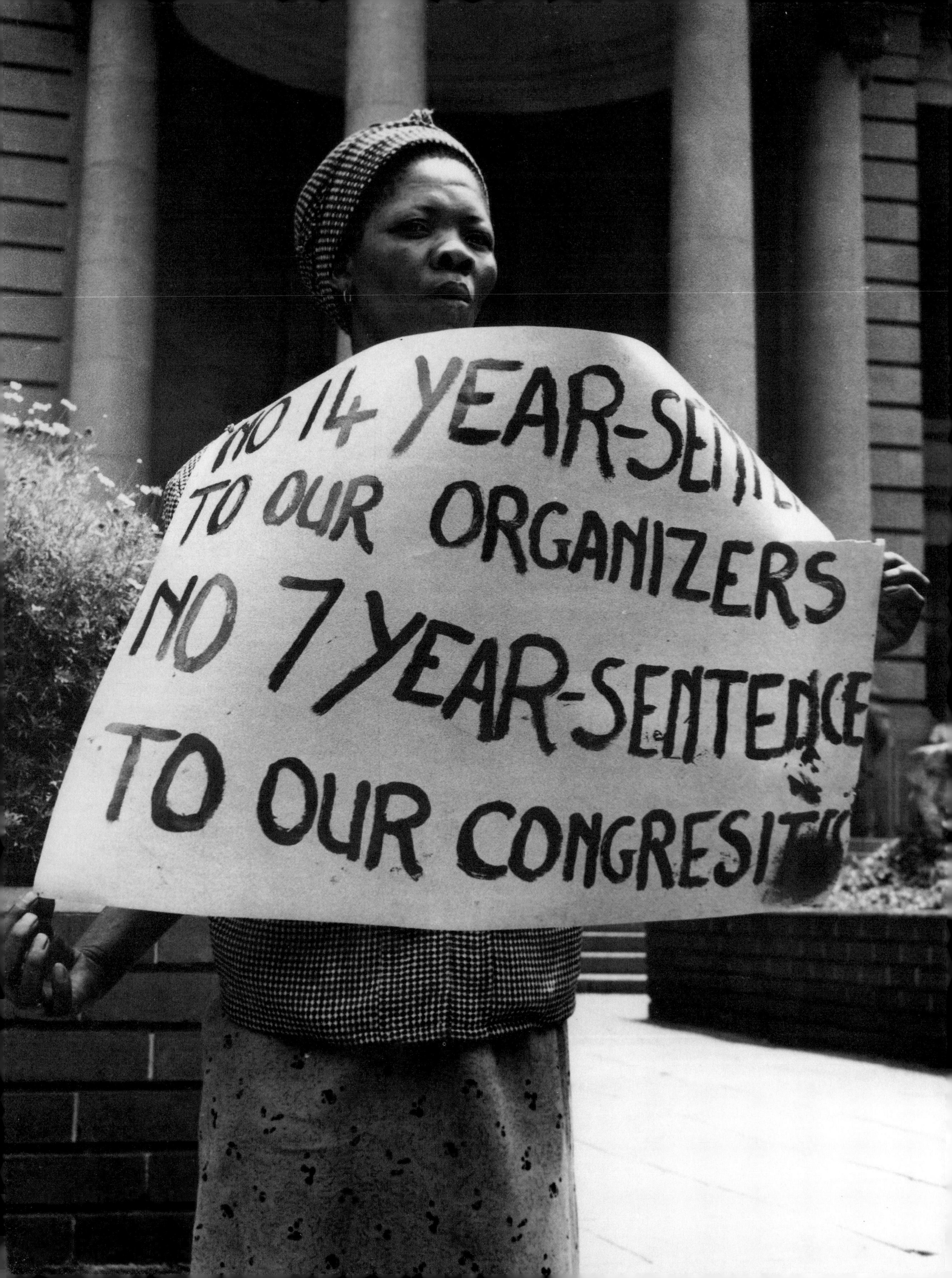
NO 14 YEAR-
TO OUR ORGANIZERS
NO 7 YEAR-SENTENCE
TO OUR

A Single Photograph, a Thousand Words

I do not know whether it was Peter Magubane's questing admiration for women in South Africa that led him to spend years of his life, and all the changes of a deepening vision of his art, on the conception of this book, or whether, in those years and impinging upon that vision, the role of women in the struggle for liberation emerged more and more inescapably in the eye of his camera. That role has been, and is, awesome. And however the focus of this book came about, the photographs between these covers capture it awesomely.

As a writer I have always rather resented the dictum that a single photograph is worth a thousand words. But studying Magubane's photographs of women — and no one who takes up this book will go through it only once — I see that the journalistic dictum can be true. There are mouths caught wide with anger and defiance, here, but the wordless defiance of endurance is captured in countless faces and body postures: in the tenderness of a gesture toward a child; in the hands, twisted as tree roots, of an old woman, too poor to buy spectacles, trying to thread a needle; in the glorious smile of a young girl with a heavy jar of water on her head, asserting life in the midst of hardship. A thousand words could not have conveyed the force of a single one of these images.

Women have assumed the burdens of resistance against oppression from far-off beginnings in the era of early white conquest, when the confusion of meeting with spears the guns of the invaders produced desperate prophecy — Nongquase, the Joan of Arc figure, with her tragic vision of the sacrifice of her people's cattle that magically would bring about the return of the whites to the sea from where they appeared. The jar of water on their heads, the load of firewood or thatching grass on their backs isn't all the women have carried. They have marched in protest on the stone towers of power, they have faced police batons, tear gas, and guns, they have been detained and tried; for to expect justice, to demand the freedom to seek work, to earn enough to feed and clothe your children, to be housed, to be educated, was for many, many years treasonable in our country.

In the 1950s, the era of civil disobedience campaigns, there emerged women leaders in the first contemporary forms of resistance. Following the tactics of *Satyagraha* (soul force) which Mahatma Gandhi as a young lawyer had worked out during his years in South Africa, African, Indian, and a number of white women entered areas segregated by law for one group or another, took part in sit-ins, defied color bar restrictions in cities. "Passive resistance" this was termed; but in South Africa there was no compact of non-violence recognized by the government: nothing passive about the mass arrests with which the police met these peaceable assertions of human rights.

Seeing the faces of some of the women in this book, I suddenly am reminded that one of my early stories, "The Smell of Death and Flowers," was about the experience of a couple of young white women joining a march and entering a black township in defiance of the law; their fears banished by the comradeship of their fellow black defiers, the curiosity of the township children, the unexpected warmth of township people. And I remember being taken to visit one of the most popular black women leaders, Lilian Ngoyi, in her strange little house in Soweto. It was one of a conglomerate which, approached from a rise, looked like the humped backs of a herd of elephant — and, indeed, these were known as the "elephant houses"; gray cement shells, they were one of the white authorities' experiments in cheap housing for the thousands of blacks from rural areas who had been welcomed to Johannesburg to man wartime industries, but excluded from white residential areas and not provided with anywhere to live.

There was nothing gray about Lilian Ngoyi, however. She rushed out to greet us with the taut bearing and lively voice of a dramatic personality, and the brightness of her clothes was in itself a defiance of the dreary township. She was as bold and fiery a speaker as any man. She moved into the next phase of resistance and was an accused in the first great Treason Trial, in 1956, along with Helen Joseph, Ruth First, Frances Baard, Bertha Mashaba, Bertha Mkize, and others. She died in old age; much that she worked for — for which Ruth First lost her life when a parcel bomb sent by an assassin exploded in her hands, for which Helen Joseph has splendidly survived all means of duress at the state's disposal — has come about. But the elephant houses are still lived in, while even now women in their thousands, crowded into squatter camps, have to make some kind of home out of plastic sheeting and cardboard.

So far as women in general are concerned, South African attitudes, like those in most societies based on colonial conquest, traditionally placed women in a supportive, secondary role, socially, and no role at all, politically. A hierarchy of domination is the very structure by which colonialism exists, and with white men at the apex, so far as human rights are concerned, white women came only just above black men, who had practically no rights, and black women came lowest of all. Women were there to bind the wounds men inflicted on one another; they were not considered capable of having any part in the decisions that determine conflict or peace, justice before the law, or the living conditions under which they were delegated to keep the home fires burning. Some white women had the dubious advantage of being pampered dolls; black women had the added disadvantage of another tradition, the submissive role expected of women by black men.

Of course, there had been "unfeminine" exceptions, de-sexed, so to speak, by their masculine presumption: women such as Nongquase and Olive Schreiner: abnormal — they must be prophetesses if black, bluestocking spinsters if white. No "real" woman would take it upon herself to tell men what to do, whether in facing conquest or whether, as Schreiner did, directing them to the shame of their racism. But with the rise of militancy in the tactics of liberation in the second half of the 1950s, black women came forward among men to meet the historical demands of their time, demands that could not be met by traditional female participation. Women black and white, from the narrowest and most convention-bound backgrounds on both sides of the color bar, became trade union leaders; a women's movement within the African National Congress and in other liberation formations surged irresistibly into action.

Magubane's photographs of the marches of women in protest against the introduction of passes that they would have to carry as men did, and which would restrict their free movement as that of men was restricted, show an awakening from the drug of male domination as epitomized in the white male government, some triumph of the achievement of full consciousness, of the dignity of speaking up for oneself instead of being spoken for — all before one's eyes, there in the doughty confrontation of those faces of heavy, worn matrons, striding young women, the sense of an eager throng jostling in the common purpose of deciding their own lives. The status the women gained for themselves was granted — ironically — by the wide police action they provoked. The police did them the honor of treating them as ruthlessly as they would have done men. And there is an eloquent image (again worth more than a thousand words!) of the stringent suppression of information, which began about that time, in the single photograph in this book *not* taken by Magubane — a colleague caught the moment when Magubane was being arrested for photographing the pass protest march of 3,500 women in the streets of Johannesburg.

The women did not succeed in having the pass laws rescinded (these were abolished only in the mid-1980s) but their role in the modern political struggle was redefined, for good, in that era of the first Treason Trial, when women were not only in the front row of demonstrators under the banner "We Stand by Our Leaders" but *were* some of the leaders on trial. At the

Sharpeville massacre in 1960, a baby was killed by a police bullet where it was tied on its mother's back; but women were no longer only the victims of, they were also the activists in, the long struggle for liberation.

Liberation has had many phases of political action. The South African white regime saw its outlawing of the liberation movements, the imprisonment or exile of leaders, as the final triumphant suppression of black aspirations. The backside of power seated itself confidently over a political fault-line like that of a geological one through which, sooner or later, an earthquake will inevitably burst forth. The uprisings that began in 1976 sent the complacency of the government and the white population flying. The revolt of black youth — boys and girls — was backed first by their mothers, and it was a woman leader, Winnie Mandela, who many times stood between them and the police. It was the women who came out of their houses into police fire carrying water and rags to wash away the tear gas burning their children's eyes. Women were binding up the wounds men had caused, yes; but they were also identifying themselves, in their own right, with the revolt of their boys and girls against discrimination in education and the entire structure of racism which denied them a future.

While women are taking part in the momentum of political action, and a growing feminist movement among young black women is adapting feminist issues, common to women all over the world, to the particular ones of South African black women in the liberation struggle, the load of firewood on the back and the jar of water on the head have not been cast off. Some of the most moving images in this book are photographs of women in the rural areas; in the artificial "statelets" created by the Verwoerd plan of the sixties to divide South Africa into developed territory for whites and undeveloped territory for blacks; in the wastelands to which black communities were moved to make room for whites. These photographs produce silence, in the viewer. In the fifties and sixties these women were contract laborers in potato fields, bearing babies to be wrapped in sacks; in the seventies and eighties they were dumped in "resettlement" areas, supplied with tin toilets and nothing else; in the nineties they are not the same women and yet they are still the same women, because the other struggle, the struggle for survival for their families, has not changed with the generations. If their lives do not change in the new South Africa to which black women, and some of their white sisters, have contributed so much sacrifice, even the presence of women in cabinet positions, if that should come, would not mean that justice for women has been achieved.

As for the final phase of the political struggle, the photographs of hostel killings, the battles between men that in the early nineties have spilled over horrifyingly to nearby houses and squatter camps and brought terror killings to commuters on trains, tell a story closer to the question of gender than you would gather from newspaper reports. Far back, behind the machinations of political rivalry, beneath the evil intentions of those who want to create a chaos of disregard for human life in which a decent society cannot be established, there is the very existence of these all-male hostels as the basis of a labor system that has deprived and brutalized men into perfect material for incitement to violence. What is not so obvious is the link with the great suffering of three generations of women. They, too, have been shackled to the migratory labor system by which South Africa's place as the most advanced country in the subcontinent has been gained. These are Magubane's "eternal grass widows." His 1959 photograph of a woman plowing because all the village men are away as contract laborers is not a period image; he could find the same subject in the rural areas today. And in the urban sprawl of "formal" housing — bricks and mortar — and "informal" housing — squatter shacks — the women and children who are driven from their shelter in the spreading terror of hostel violence are also the victims of the migratory labor system, for it goes back to the early years of the century, and the colonial ethos that black men and women, black families, don't need each other as white men and women, white families, do.

The tragedy of black women's lives, the incredible resistance and resilience that has somehow enabled them to overcome defeat, thrust their dignity in the face of degradation and abuse, keep their lovingness alive against hate, are there in the faces and bodies of this book, in the slim beauty turning her back on the hostile, staring street and in the time-folded face of an old woman. At the rendezvous of victory, to which we now draw near, the women in this book have earned their rightful place.

— Nadine Gordimer

Life under Apartheid and the
Roots of the Struggle

The sun shone hot the afternoon that Beauty Qabela, an eighteen-year-old with a sunbeam smile, went to buy a carton of milk for her employer. Beauty worked as a nanny, caring for Doreen Wilson's four-year-old son, Timmy. It was a short walk to the corner café, and Beauty hummed as she strode along the tree-lined pavement in the white Johannesburg suburb of Fairview. Suddenly, a police van screeched to a halt beside her.

"Pass, where's your pass?" shouted the young white policeman as he jumped from the vehicle. Armed and aggressive, he towered above the frightened girl. "Hey, girl, show me your pass," he snarled.

Silently, Beauty handed him her reference book.

"There's no stamp," he snorted. "There's no damn stamp. What are you doing here without a stamp?"

Roughly he jerked Beauty to the back of the barred van, opened the door, and threw her inside. Her left leg thumped against the sharp metal edge and the skin peeled away, leaving a bloody gash.

Inside, eight African women sat silently, their eyes sympathetic. "Sit here, sister," said a grandmother, her hair white, her face wrinkled. Shifting along the mean seat, she made space for Beauty.

As the police van gathered speed, the women spoke softly among themselves. "Courage, sister," said one. "It will be our turn one day, but we will not be such animals."

The women were herded into a cell at the local police station. That night, they slept on the cement floor without mattresses or blankets and they huddled together for warmth.

The following morning, Beauty and her companions were driven in a police vehicle to the Johannesburg Magistrate's Court, where, taking her turn with several hundred other arrested women, she appeared before a magistrate. It took less than five minutes for Beauty to become a criminal. Charged under Section 10 (1) of the Blacks (Urban Areas) Consolidation Act, she was found guilty and fined thirty rand (approximately ten dollars) or fifteen days in jail.

Her crime? Being where she was without official permission. Her pass was "not in order." Had it been correctly stamped, she would have been able to live and work in Fairview.

Movement of Africans in South Africa was, at this time (1976), heavily restricted and they were confined to certain areas. In order to live or work elsewhere, permission had to be granted by the authorities. That permission was given only under very specific circumstances. If permission was granted, the pass book, which had to be carried by all Africans over the age of sixteen, was stamped by government authorities. Blacks were subjected to frequent searches by the police to ensure they were not in an area without stamped permission. The law stated that no African person was allowed to stay for longer than seventy-two hours in an urban area unless he or she had special permission to be there, and it was against the law for anyone to employ an African who did not have the correct official stamp. Thus, hundreds and thousands of Africans were denied the opportunity to move or work freely in the land of their birth. Some sympathetic whites, such as Doreen Wilson, nevertheless employed these people illegally; if they were caught, they too were fined. But because of the system, there were also unscrupulous employers who hired "illegal" Africans and exploited them by paying low wages. Women, desperate for work, took poorly paid jobs and worked for a few rand a month.

Beauty Qabela did not have the money to pay the fine, so she was jailed. On release, she was sent back to her village near Standerton in the Transvaal, where drought and poor soil had stunted the crops and made the cattle as gaunt as the people. She returned to the small hut where her remaining four sisters and brothers and five cousins were cared for by their elderly grandmother. That year, two siblings had died from malnutrition. The year before, her mother and youngest sister had died of tuberculosis and her father had been shot dead while running from the police. They said he'd stolen a car, but he'd never even learned to drive — the transport of his youth had been a skinny horse.

Beauty Qabela was the sole support of her ever-hungry family. A young woman with five years of primary school education, fluent in Zulu, with a smattering of English and Afrikaans, but having a pass book that lacked a stamp permitting her to work in Johannesburg, she nevertheless returned to "Egoli," the City of Gold, as Johannesburg is called by many Africans, to work illegally as an unskilled domestic. In the ten years until 1986, when the repressive influx control laws were abolished, Beauty was arrested and endorsed out of Johannesburg ten times. Each time she returned and found a job with a sympathetic employer who would hire her even though she was an "illegal." Beauty Qabela, a wisp of a girl with a smile like a sunbeam and the courage of a lioness, supported and educated her entire family.

The story of Beauty Qabela epitomizes the struggle of the African women of South Africa. It is a story of indefatigable courage and inspiration and demonstrates the ability of ordinary women to fight against all odds and overcome.

Oppressed by repressive apartheid laws, tyrannized by tribal laws, discriminated against in every facet of life, black women are the most persecuted people in a country not known for its human rights record. *Black* is the term preferred by South African people of color and is used to describe Africans, coloreds, and Asians. In South African political terms, *African* describes indigenous negroid black people, *colored* refers to people of mixed race, and *Asians* are mostly Indians whose forefathers came to South Africa from India as indentured laborers.

Over the years, like many tributory streams, African, Indian, colored, and a few white South African women came together and formed a mighty flowing river of hope and determination. Together they fought for freedom and dignity, for equal rights and justice. For over eighty-two years, from the Act of Union in 1909 until today, they have strived to make a better land for their children, to give them what they never had, the right to be free in their own country, to receive education, to live in dignity. Impoverished, imprisoned, denigrated, brutalized, and abused, they refused to be vanquished.

South Africa's womanhood, the heart and spirit of the nation, resisted oppression fiercely. "*Wathinta abafazi, wathint' imbokodo, uzakufa* — Strijdom, you have tampered with the women, you have struck a rock, you will die [he did]" are the stirring words of a protest song composed on that momentous and historical day, August 9, 1956, when twenty thousand women marched on the seat of government in Pretoria. (J. G. Strijdom was then prime minister of the country.) They had come from all over South Africa to demonstrate against an impending apartheid law, the draconian legislation that would make it compulsory for African women to carry pass books.

Today, South Africa is in a state of transition. The apartheid state is crumbling; discriminatory apartheid laws have been repealed; Nelson Mandela, president of the African National Congress (ANC), has been released from prison, as have most other political prisoners. Formerly banned liberation movements and political parties have been unbanned — the ANC, the South African Communist Party (SACP), formerly the Communist Party of South Africa (CPSA), the Pan-Africanist Congress (PAC) — and political exiles are returning. Slowly, the country is democratizing.

By the end of the nineteenth century, white settlers, who originated from Holland, France, England, and Germany, had conquered what is today called South Africa and the blacks, the conquered, became laborers — on farms, in cities, in mines. In 1899 and 1902, the British defeated the Afrikaners (then Dutch-speaking, today Afrikaans-speaking) in the Anglo-Boer Wars. The prime cause of war was that the British wanted control of the subcontinent, which included rich diamond and gold resources. The Boers fiercely defended their independence from the most extensive empire in the history of the world, but in vain. In 1910, the four British colonies — the Cape, Transvaal, Orange Free State, and Natal — formed the Union of South Africa. Aside from a small group of colored men in the Cape who were allowed to retain the franchise because they met certain economic and educational requirements, blacks were denied the franchise, as were all women. Whites were supreme, and thus racist South Africa was born.

Since 1910, successive governments have pursued policies and initiated laws designed to segregate blacks and whites with the intention of keeping whites, the minority, in power over the black majority. (Of a population of approximately thirty million people, only four million are whites.)

The legislation prejudicial against blacks took many forms. One example was the passing in 1913 and 1936 of the Land Acts, which reserved only 13 percent of South Africa for blacks to live on. Migrant labor has been enforced in South Africa since the turn of the century. When the presently ruling National Party (NP) came to power in 1948, it introduced additional laws to ensure the absolute supremacy of whites. Blacks, disenfranchised and dispossessed, were increasingly moved from their land by the minority government, whose apartheid legislation was the foundation for economic growth in serving the labor needs of the white community.

Influx control measures, the Group Areas Act, the Immorality Act (by which sex across the color bar, mixed marriage, or the mixing of races was forbidden), the Population Registration Act, job reservation for specified races (superior jobs for whites, menial jobs for blacks), the Bantu Education Act (designed to keep blacks as laborers) — each shameful piece of legislation was designed to keep whites in power and blacks suppressed.

According to African tradition, women were inferior in status (they were regarded as minors) and this was entrenched by tribal law. Yet indirectly, the law under apartheid caused an ironic reversal of African women's status. Forced to become the heads of their families when their men left to work as migrant laborers in the cities for months on end, they assumed the responsibilities of their absent men. They built their dwellings, supported their families, and farmed the lands. When their husbands left to work in the mines or in the cities, they became the backbone of the nation, keeping the home fires burning literally and figuratively. Whole communities became matriarchal, with the exception of the brief periods when the menfolk temporarily returned.

With the industrialization of South Africa and the consequent growth of towns, economic circumstance forced rural African women to abandon their traditional lifestyle. Younger women left their children with elderly relatives and traveled to the cities seeking work.

The system of pass laws, an effective form of influx control, tore families apart. Forbidden by law to bring their children to urban areas, mothers and children would be separated for long periods. That pattern still exists today. With their fathers already working as migrant laborers, children were virtually orphaned when their mothers left as well. Grandmothers, aged aunts, and baby-minders looked after the children of the absent parents. Distances were great, communications poor, and the small sums of money sent home to feed the families often did not reach them. Children died of starvation, illness, and sometimes neglect. Even today, South Africa has one of the highest infant mortality rates in the world.

From the formation of the Union of South Africa in 1910 until the abolition of the pass laws in 1986, the implementation of those laws was one of the prime methods used by the government to control the African population. Black women were exempted from carrying passes until 1956 except in the Orange Free State, where, since 1910, provincial laws required both African men and women to carry passes. The first organized political protest by African women took place in 1913, when the women of the Orange Free State protested against having to carry these passes.

As a direct result of the 1913 Orange Free State antipass campaign, the Bantu

Women's League, part of the ANC, was formed. The women, auxiliary members of the ANC, had restricted status. However, under the presidency of Charlotte Maxeke, the league took up the issue of pass laws. She was one of the few African women of that time with a tertiary education, a B.Sc. degree from the United States. Tireless in the struggle against the injustices perpetrated upon her people by a racist government, Charlotte Maxeke believed women should work together with their men to improve the situation. Gradually women joined the struggle and in 1928 in Potchefstroom, Transvaal, the league, led by Josie Palmer, also a CPSA member, demonstrated against the issuing of residential permits to Africans.

Africans have always viewed with repugnance the idea of legislation forcing their women to carry passes, with resulting punishment and imprisonment if they do not. "Jail our women and our families will suffer" has been the vociferous opposition cry over the years. Tragically, this has been proved — time and time again.

Pass laws in one form or another, requiring African men to carry passes as their form of identification, and so permitting them to live and work only in certain areas, have been a form of control exercised on the African population since the nineteenth century. In 1910, with the formation of Union, pass laws were extended, and in 1913, the Land Act restricting African ownership of land formed the basis of the policy of migrant labor.

In the 1920s and 1930s, pass legislation restricting the movement of African men was expanded — women were still not considered an important economic force. In 1930 and 1937, municipalities were empowered to prevent African women from entering their areas to look for work. Finally, in 1956, women were included in the all-embracing and rigid legislation.

When this pass law for women was eventually pushed through Parliament by the National Party government, hundreds of black women were imprisoned throughout the country. They were arrested because they resisted and refused to carry passes. However, eventually all African women were forced to register and acquire passes. In the 1960s and 1970s, thousands of women were arrested when they moved illegally around the country desperately seeking work. The tragedy and suffering caused by these inhumane laws was inestimable.

In the twenties, thirties, and forties, white women were concerned with the issue of suffrage because women had no vote. Black women, on the other hand, became politically active within recognized liberation movements fighting against white supremacy — the ANC, the African People's Organisation (APO), the

Communist Party of South Africa (CPSA), the Pan-Africanist Congress, and various trade unions. During this time, these movements did not have the strength they acquired in later years. Men were primarily the activists. However, black women, especially Africans, coloreds, and Indians, worked alongside their men in opposing oppression and discrimination.

During the 1930s, women were mainly active in trade union movements. In fact, the trade unions were the force that galvanized the women into action. In July 1931, it was the garment workers on the Witwatersrand, again mainly women, who came out in strike as a protest against the proposed pass curfews that were to be imposed on Africans. The strike in Johannesburg and the surrounding areas was a great success and it helped pave the way for the formation of a national women's movement. The most prominent woman trade unionist was Ray Alexander, who had arrived in 1929 as a fifteen-year-old immigrant from Latvia, where she had experienced firsthand oppression against Latvian Jews. Almost immediately upon her arrival in South Africa, she became involved in political issues and joined the CPSA. She played a constructive role in the struggle against racial discrimination, and in industry she campaigned ceaselessly for women's rights. It was Ray Alexander who established the Food and Canning Workers Union (FCWU) in 1941. An active union, it campaigned for the rights of workers — most of whom were women. She stressed the need for women to organize themselves into an effective organization of their own.

Alexander was instrumental in the formation of the Federation of South African Women. A tireless worker, her popularity grew and she traveled the country campaigning for the planned inaugural conference of a proposed federation of women. In 1954 she stood in a parliamentary by-election as Native (African people's) Representative in the Cape Western Division. She won the election by an overwhelming majority, but was prevented from taking her seat by the Nationalist government, which declared the elections invalid. The previous incumbent, Brian Bunting, had been expelled from the House of Assembly in terms of the Suppression of Communism Act and they were determined that another Communist would not take the seat.

Dora Mabonela's hands are dry and callused and as hard as sun-dried leather. Now in her eighties, she suffers from arthritis of the finger joints, probably the result of working as a washerwoman for the past sixty-eight years.

Born in 1911 in old Sophiatown on the edge of Johannesburg when it was still an African freehold area (one of the few places in the country where Africans could own land), she was eleven when she began washing white people's clothes. She'd leave home in the early morning darkness and on an empty stomach walk for three and a half hours to arrive at the "madam's" house before 7 A.M.

Washing and scrubbing by hand on a corrugated washboard, she was satisfied only when each garment sparkled. Then she'd stand for hours, ironing clothes stiffly starched to perfection. For lunch she was given weak tea and bread. Sugar was rationed — never more than two spoonfuls per cup — and if she was lucky she'd be given the occasional leftovers, which she'd hide in a large cloth bag she carried under her arm.

For ten hours of work she was paid a few shillings. As the years passed, things improved, but not much. There were washing machines and electric irons, and transport to and from work became more frequent. But she still had to leave before sunrise to get to work on time. And always she arrived home after dark. Today, thousands of black women stream from the townships to work in white areas in exactly the same way.

Dora eventually married and had five children. Each time she was pregnant she worked until just a few days before the birth of the baby. A week after the birth, she'd bring the tiny infant to work tied on her back with a blanket. An elderly aunt cared for the young children she left at home. Her husband, a laborer on construction sites, became ill with tuberculosis and eventually died, so to support her family, she took in mending to earn extra income.

In 1954, under the Group Areas Act, Sophiatown was proclaimed a white area and blacks were forcibly removed. Under this act, individuals were, on the grounds of race, restricted to owning property in specific state-demarcated areas of a town and excluded from all others. Even established businesses were forced to move if in the wrong group area. Under the Group Areas Act, a man who had built his house might be forced to leave it and his children would be unable to inherit it because it was suddenly in the wrong racial group area. Almost always, it was blacks who were forced to move to make way for whites.

In place of Sophiatown was built Triomf (the Afrikaans word for *triumph*), a particularly insensitive name for a white town built on the tragedy and misery of its former black inhabitants. The hardship suffered by those who were evicted and forced to give up the homes they and their families had lived in for generations was immense. The bitterness and suffering caused by this act, not repealed until 1990, is just one of the legacies of apartheid.

Dora Mabonela and her family moved to the newly developed South Western townships, more commonly known as Soweto. Soweto, today a sprawling ghetto, home to three million blacks, was originally built as a township for the relocation of blacks who had been ousted from their homes under the Group Areas Act. In Sophiatown, the Mabonelas had electricity and taps with hot and cold water. There were good schools in the vicinity — this was prior to the government's enforcement of the Bantu Education Act of 1953, which ensured that blacks received inferior education. Most important of all, the Mabonelas were surrounded by close friends and a supportive community.

In Soweto there was no electricity, the houses were Spartan and small with bare, concrete floors and tin roofs, and outside was a cold-water tap and a toilet per household. In some places, like Pimville, the night soil system prevailed. The dung cart moved in broad daylight collecting buckets of excrement. The unpleasant stench blanketed the air. Although Dora was barely literate, her children attended high school and then studied further. Proudly she would boast of her three schoolteacher children and of her last-born, a nurse. For most of their youth they studied by candlelight, as it was only in the mid-1970s that Dora Mabonela's family acquired electricity. Despite being a simple washerwoman, Dora educated her children and gave them opportunities she'd been denied.

It is 1978 and, like many others in a similar situation, this seventy-five-year-old woman from Jabavu cares for her grandson while his parents are at work. She's worried because he refuses to attend school.

16

Threading a needle is difficult at the best of times, but when you're old and cannot afford to buy a pair of spectacles, it becomes an almost impossible feat. Granny Cele is seen in 1968 preparing to sew a dress for her youngest grandchild.

OPPOSITE: A quick on-site repair. While his mother worked in the white suburbs as a domestic, this small boy was cared for by his grandmother in a township called Pimville, which in 1962 consisted of corrugated iron shacks. When his pants split, she popped him over her knee and stitched the tear together.

These are the hands of an illiterate washerwoman who washed white people's clothes for thirty years. Each day, she'd leave home in Soweto in the 4 A.M. darkness to journey across town to work and return home well after night had fallen. Her pay was minimal, but some of the best-educated young blacks of today achieved their education with money made by these means.

In 1967, the Mzumba
dancers of Soweto,
in traditional Zulu
costume, appeared
onstage to entertain
audiences with their
spirited tribal dancing.

This woman had been
brought to Delmas
from the Transkei to
work in the potato
fields. Picking potatoes
was backbreaking
work, and at night she
slept on potato sacks.
During the week, she
existed on mealie
meal; as a special
treat, the farmer pro-
vided his workers with
a pig's head once a
week.

A *sangoma*, a traditional medicine woman, throws the bones and consults her ancestors to solve a patient's problem. *Sangomas* are held in high regard by people who believe in their mystical powers.

Today, initiation ceremonies are more common in the rural areas, but in 1978, these young girls from the urban township of Evaton, just outside Johannesburg, took part in a traditional ceremony to initiate them into womanhood.

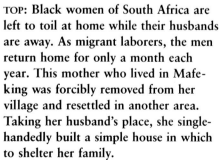

TOP: Black women of South Africa are left to toil at home while their husbands are away. As migrant laborers, the men return home for only a month each year. This mother who lived in Mafeking was forcibly removed from her village and resettled in another area. Taking her husband's place, she single-handedly built a simple house in which to shelter her family.

BOTTOM: In 1959, during the unrest in Pondoland, Peter Magubane was present when this woman's house was burned down. Said Magubane: "I watched her home burn, but there was nothing we could do. Eventually, we were told by the police we'd have to leave, otherwise we'd be arrested. She and her small children were left with nothing." She built a temporary shelter from the remains of her house in which to protect her children from the cold night air.

This young Pondo woman is tilling her fields during her husband's absence.

OVERLEAF: A Diepkloof mother and child rest in their modest match-box house. These houses have no ceilings or inside doors, nor do they have running water or any other modern facilities.

As elegant as a
flamingo, this Ndebele
woman walks from
her small village to the
nearest township to
sell her homemade
brooms.

At Nqutu, among the
rolling hills of Natal,
the villagers live in
small mud and grass
huts that cling to the
hillside. Each day this
Zulu mother walked a
mile to fetch water
from a stream. The
journey home was
always more difficult
because of the weight
of the filled barrel.
The photograph was
taken in 1978.

In 1978, these women
from the Transkei
worked as contract
laborers in the potato
fields of Kinross in the
Eastern Transvaal.
Because their contracts
were for nine-month
periods, their children
grew up motherless,
cared for by elderly
relatives.

In 1977, a young girl
is whipped by the
makgotla (an infor-
mal, kangaroo court in
Soweto, which was
hated by the commu-
nity but supported by
the police). Residents
were persecuted by
these self-imposed
courts and the punish-
ment meted out was
often brutal.

A young Alexandra
township mother heat-
ing water on a Primus
stove to prepare break-
fast for her children.

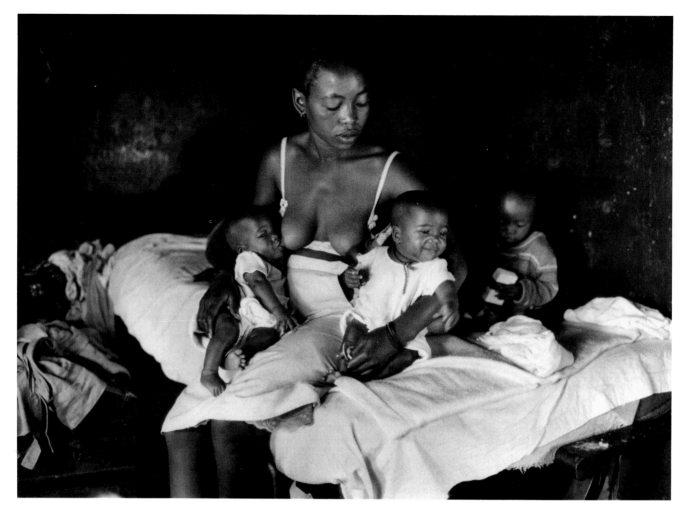

This young mother
lived with her husband
and three small chil-
dren in a one-room tin
shack in Alexandra
township. The com-
munity cold-water tap
and the toilet were
outside at the end of
the yard.

Traditionally, white
South African children
are brought up by
black nannies who live
in separate quarters
within the family's
home. These women
love and care for their
charges, but often
don't see their own
children for months.
A youngster and her
nanny enjoy a day in
the park. In the days
of the Separate Ameni-
ties Act, even park
benches were restricted
for different race
groups.

1940s–1950s: The Formation of the ANC Women's League through the Johannesburg Pass Protests

The 1940s and 1950s — the latter decade marking the start of this photographic documentation — were the decades in which the women of South Africa first recognized their common struggle and organized to combat the forces against them. It was during these years that solely female political groups first emerged in significant numbers. There was a new awareness at work — the awareness that the experience of women under apartheid demanded its own voice. Women emerged at the forefront as political leaders. They raised their voices against the many forms of oppression that so crippled their lives and those of their families: lack of housing, food shortages, and the pass laws. In these years their protest, coming from ever deeper grass-roots support, was characterized by passionate nonviolence.

During the war years of the 1940s, the various liberation movements maintained a low profile. The United Party, under General Jan Christiaan Smuts, seemed more relaxed than previous governments, but in effect, the lot of blacks was not improved.

In 1943, the ANC Women's League (ANCWL) was formed with Madie-Hall Xuma as its first president. An American university graduate, she was the wife of Dr. A. B. Xuma, president of the ANC. Meanwhile, Indian women joined the struggle as members of the South African Indian Congress (SAIC). Though the number of Indian women activists was small in the forties and fifties, they made their presence felt. Dr. Kaisevello Goonam, a prominent SAIC member, along with Fatima Meer and Mrs. N. P. Desai, were instrumental in leading the Passive Resistance Campaign of 1946 and 1947. This campaign strongly demonstrated against the legislation that restricted the freedom of movement of the Indian people. At that time, Indians were not allowed to move from one province to another without a permit. As a protest, Indian activists crossed the border from Natal into the Transvaal and over two thousand were arrested and jailed.

Amina Cachalia, a young activist, formed the Progressive Women's Union in an attempt to teach Indian women to become more independent of their economic and social restraints. The intention of the Progressive Women's Union was to equip Indian women with self-help skills such as typing and sewing. Her father had been chairman of the Indian Congress during the Gandhi period, so Amina Cachalia grew up in a politicized home. Although too young to participate actively in the Passive Resistance Campaign, she supported the Defiance Campaign of 1952. One of the most brutal apartheid laws was the statute empowering a government minister to ban an individual on the basis of certain acts, such as the Suppression of Communism Act of 1950. The banning statute enabled a minister to publish a notice banning or placing a person under house arrest. Amina Cachalia was banned for fifteen years, from 1963 until 1978, and under her banning order was allowed to see only three people, one at a time.

When the National Party came to power in 1948, it quickly enforced apartheid, and more encompassing discriminatory laws were introduced to ensure the supremacy of whites.

At this time, African women began making their voices heard by organizing grass-roots campaigns about issues that affected them. For example, in Alexandra township and Evaton in the Vaal Triangle they joined a bus boycott to protest against the increase in the price of bus tickets. From dusk to dawn, township dwellers walked long distances to and from work. Nurses would leave home shortly after midnight to be able to arrive at their hospitals on time. Even mothers, with babies tied to their backs in traditional African style, walked ten or fifteen miles, exhausted and hungry, but refusing the easier option of catching a bus. The boycott was successful, and bus tickets reverted to their old price. In the Cape, a Women's Food Committee was formed to demonstrate against the rising price of food.

The chronic shortage of housing was another of the many problems facing Africans. To the chagrin of the authorities, temporary squatter camps sprung up everywhere and eventually became permanent — people had nowhere else to live. Nevertheless, the government tried to obliterate them. Whole communities would be forcibly removed by the authorities, who entered the camps with bulldozers and trucks, knocking down and destroying shacks when people refused to leave voluntarily.

Squatters were forced to load the trucks with their belongings and were then taken to a designated place for resettlement. Often these new areas were remote, far from any built-up towns where blacks might find employment, and often there were no facilities available for those removed.

Women became increasingly involved in squatter movements, fiercely demonstrating against removals, and in 1947 they marched through Johannesburg protesting against the shortage of housing for Africans.

Dora Tamana, a well-known activist of the time, was instrumental in organizing a march of Johannesburg women of all colors on International Women's Day on March 8, 1947. Tamana's family came from a small village in the Transkei, and she'd grown up with firsthand knowledge of terrible poverty. Each day she walked half a mile to fetch water from a spring. She had four years of schooling and grew up helping her parents on their smallholding. She married, and when her husband left for Cape Town as a migrant laborer, she moved to Queenstown, where she struggled to exist. Three of her four babies died before she eventually joined her husband in Cape Town. She became politicized through bitter experience, and in later years headed the All-Women's Union, one of the first attempts to form a national women's movement.

It was in the 1950s that women truly became a force in the liberation struggle. Under the National Party, apartheid was entrenched and the lives of all blacks, especially Africans, were governed by laws designed to make and keep them subservient to whites.

The country seethed with unrest. Events forced the ANC into an activist role, and in 1952, the movement launched a country-wide Defiance Campaign of civil disobedience against the government. Blacks were arrested in the thousands as they ignored repressive laws, and women were prominent in this campaign.

In 1953, the ANC, the SAIC, the Coloured People's Congress, and the Congress of Democrats (COD) formed the Congress Alliance. The South African Congress of Trade Unions (COSATU) joined the Alliance two years later. The Congress Alliance espoused a policy of passive resistance to mount its many campaigns.

This was the time of women such as Annie Silinga, described by South African author and journalist Anthony Sampson, now living in London, as a "veteran battle-ax." Even when passes were made statutory for women, Annie Silinga refused to carry one until the day she died. A gutsy fighter, she was the first African woman to sit in a "whites-only" waiting room at a station. At the time she said: "We defied bad laws."

Annie Silinga's spirit never dimmed. One of the organizers of the Defiance Campaign, she remained an activist all her life. A simple woman, born in the Transkei, her courage was legendary and her beliefs steadfast. Refusing to carry the hated pass, she was denied an old-age pension. Although that pension was nominal and far less than the old-age pension for whites, for many it meant the difference between starvation and survival. Annie Silinga was fortunate to have loving children who cared for her in her old age.

The laws enforcing apartheid — the Urban Areas Act, the Group Areas Act, the Bantu Education Act — were all designed to keep whites dominant. Women demonstrated alongside their men to protest these laws, and in 1954, encouraged by several activists of different liberation movements, decided to pool their resources in the struggle for liberation. On the weekend of April 17, 1954, women from all over the country joined together to form the embryonic Federation of South African Women (FSAW). Their aims were based on a Women's Charter with a policy that stated: "This organisation is formed for the purpose of uniting all women in common action for the removal of all political, legal, economic and social disabilities."

Says Cherryl Walker in *Women and Resistance in South Africa:*

> The Women's Charter was the first comprehensive statement of principles by the new women's movement. . . . The charter drew together the experience of women within the national liberation movement over the previous 40 years and mapped out the direction the leaders of the conference hoped the new organisation would take.

The first national executive read like the *Who's Who* of women activists. President was Ida Mtwana; vice-presidents were Gladys Smith, Lilian Ngoyi, Bertha Mkize, and Florence Matomela. The secretary was Ray Alexander; the treasurer, Hetty McLeod. On the committee were Frances Baard, Hettie du Preez, K. Egelhof, Christina Jasson, Helen Joseph, Elizabeth Mafeking, Fatima Meer, Louisa Mtawana, Connie Njongwe, Cecelia Rosier, Annie Silinga, Winifred Siqwana, Albertina Sisulu, Dora Tamana, Miss M. F. Thompson, Freda van Rheede, Hilda Watts (Bernstein), and Katie White.

The following year, in 1955, six white women formed the Defence of the Constitution League (DCL) — Ruth Foley, Jean Sinclair, Jean Bosazza, Helen Newton Thompson, Tercia Pybus, and Elizabeth MacLaren. It was established as a result of anger over the bill promulgated by the government to remove the colored voters of the Cape from the common voter's role, and they called upon all white women — both English- and Afrikaans-speaking — to protest against the government's destruction of the existing constitution.

They organized several demonstrations against the government, and when demonstrating always wore distinctive black mourning sashes; thus the DCL became known as the Black Sash. The Black Sash, today not a racially affiliated group, has always fought for the ideals of democracy. Although originally concerned primarily with white politics, in the thirty-seven years since its inception the Black Sash has become increasingly involved in grass-roots issues. It has several community projects, including advice centers set up throughout the country, to help the oppressed. The Black Sash deals with countless tragedies and problems, all resulting from the policy of apartheid. Detention without trial, forced removals, pass offenses, township violence, hunger relief, aid for squatters, legal aid for the underprivileged — ceaselessly, the Black Sash helps those in need.

In 1955, the government announced that from January 1, 1956, all African women would be issued passes. There was outrage. A proposed pass system for women was the final straw; Indian, white, and colored members of the women's movement decided to protest in solidarity with their African sisters.

On October 27, 1955, the FSAW organized their first march on the Union Buildings, the government headquarters in Pretoria. Harassed by the police and the authorities, two thousand women finally managed to make their way to the steps of the Union Buildings to protest against this latest iniquity. They were led by four FSAW leaders — Lilian Ngoyi, an African, Helen Joseph, a white, Rahima Moosa, an Indian, and Sophie Williams, a colored. Said Helen Joseph in her autobiography, *Side by Side:* "We reflected the multi-racial membership of the Federation of South African Women." The leaders managed to evade the police and place hundreds of signed protests at various ministers' doors. As Joseph describes the protest:

> "We have not come here to beg or plead but to ask for what is our right as mothers, as women, as citizens of our country. . . . We speak from our hearts as mothers, as women. Life cannot be stopped. We must love and marry and find a home. We must bear children in hope and in pain. We must love them as part of ourselves. We must help them grow, we must endure all the longings and sufferings of motherhood. Because of this we are made strong to come here, to speak for our children, to strive for their future.
>
> "We the voters and the voteless, call upon you, Ministers responsible for these Acts, and upon the government and the electorate of South Africa to hearken unto us."

This protest demonstration of 1955 was the first major triumph for the FSAW and the antipass campaign. Throughout the country, antipass meetings were held, and in March 1956, the FSAW decided to demonstrate in Pretoria once again in the hope that the government would be moved by the pleas of the women.

Helen Joseph and Bertha Mashaba, an executive member of the FSAW and ANC Women's League, left on a nationwide tour to drum up the support of the women and persuade them to march on Pretoria. They were accompanied by Robert Resha of the ANC and Norman Levy of the Congress of Democrats. They campaigned tirelessly, holding meetings in towns and villages and visiting women's organizations to spread their message.

The response was overwhelming. On August 9, 1956, twenty thousand women gathered on the steps of the Union Building. They had come from all over South Africa, by bus, by train, by car, and many had walked. They had traveled from Cape Town and Pofadder, from Durban and Stinkfontein, across thousands of miles. The women were young and old, some with babies on their backs, and they came from all walks of life. It was a momentous occasion, and one that has inspired South African women ever since.

Albertina Sisulu, activist and wife of Walter Sisulu, present vice-president of the ANC, recollects: "As we marched, we collected women. We arranged to meet at Pretoria Station. Our men walked beside us to support us, Nelson [Mandela] and Walter [Sisulu], they all accompanied us. When we arrived, the police announced from a loudspeaker that our march was banned.

"However, we decided to have our meeting. Instead of marching as a group, we walked in ones, twos, and threes to the Union Building. I couldn't believe what I saw when I arrived. There was a sea of women, a huge mass, oh, it was wonderful. We were so excited. We couldn't believe we were there, and so many of us. Our leaders, Lilian Ngoyi, Helen Joseph, Sophie Williams, and Rahima Moosa attempted to give our protests to the prime Minister, J. G. Strijdom, but when we got there, he'd left, he'd run away.

"When the four women returned, we stood in silent protest for thirty minutes and then started singing 'Nkosi Sikeleli Afrika' [God Bless Africa]. Twenty thousand women singing 'Nkosi Sikeleli Afrika,' you should have heard the sound of the echoes in the Union Building. There was nothing like that sound, it filled the world. Then we sang a song of the women, 'Strijdom, wathinta abafazi, wathint' imbokoda, uzakufa — Strijdom, you have tampered with the women, you have struck a rock, you have unleashed a boulder, you will die.'"

Shortly after this successful march, Lilian Ngoyi was made national president of the FSAW and Helen Joseph, national secretary. Both were dynamic leaders. They came from widely divergent backgrounds, but both were vigorous supporters of the struggle. Lilian Ngoyi, with only one year of high school education because of her family's limited resources, was self-educated, while Helen Joseph was a university graduate. Ngoyi came from a disadvantaged background, whereas Joseph had grown up as a privileged white colonialist. Although Ngoyi is remembered for her participation with national politics, it was as a garment worker that she rose to fame. Over the years, both women were harassed, banned, detained, and tried for treason (the case was eventually dismissed). Joseph was under house arrest for nine years. When the nine years expired, she was placed under banning orders for a further seven years. During the period of house arrest, she was unable to leave her house at night or weekends and was allowed no visitors. Her freedom of movement was totally restricted, as were her contact and communication with people. Under banning orders, she had no restricted hours, but in every other respect, it was virtually the same as house arrest.

Helen Joseph was still under house arrest in 1971 when she discovered she was suffering from cancer. Hospitalized for major cancer surgery, the state refused to allow her to have a friend stay with her on her discharge from the hospital. In her book, *Side by Side*, she writes: "Helen Suzman, still fighting her gallant and lonely battle in Parliament as the lone Progressive Party MP, came to see me in hospital. She had approached the Minister of Justice, Jimmy Kruger, for the lifting of my house arrest at this critical time in my life. He commented that even if I lost both arms and legs I should still be a nuisance. He would not commit himself." Shortly after this, Joseph's restriction orders were suspended, and she was free for the first time in nearly ten years.

Lilian Ngoyi was banned and remained a listed Communist until her death in 1980. When she died, she was without doubt the best-known and best-loved woman in black politics. A keen feminist, she once told a crowd: "We don't want men who wear skirts under their trousers. If they don't want to act, let us women exchange skirts with them."

Said one speaker making a tribute at her funeral: "She bore her life with dignity and harassment, detention and jail."

In December 1956, 156 anti-apartheid leaders were arrested and charged with treason. The notorious Treason Trial dragged on for four and a half years. Thirty

people were finally brought to trial, but were all acquitted in 1961. Of those originally arrested, twenty were women, including such well-known activists as Helen
Joseph, Bertha Mashaba, Lilian Ngoyi, Ruth First, Annie Silinga, Frances Baard,
and Christina Jasson. The women were in good company, for among the arrested
were Nelson Mandela, today president of the ANC, Walter Sisulu, today vice-
president of the ANC, Joe Slovo, national chairman of the South African
Communist Party, Oliver Tambo, the respected and venerable ANC leader, Professor
Z. K. Matthews, the first African to graduate from a university in South Africa,
and Albert Luthuli, president of the ANC.

During the years of the trial, women came by the thousands to offer support.
They would mass outside the Johannesburg Drill Hall, where the Treason Trial
was being held, sing, raise their fists in the traditional ANC freedom gesture, and
shout, *"Amandla"* (power), followed by *"Ngawetu"* (it is ours).

As the 1950s progressed, resistance by the women grew stronger. A mark of
that protest was its pacifist nature. Women were committed to bringing about
change by peaceful means. Slowly, the government enforced the law that women
carry passes, and women continued to resist. In October 1958, several hundred
women from different parts of Johannesburg marched upon the native commissioner's offices in Fordsburg, determined that women would under no circumstances carry passes. Their sisters from neighboring townships joined them.
Defiantly they demanded to be arrested, and within a week almost two thousand
filled the jails in central Johannesburg.

Together they marched to the native commissioner's offices; together they
refused to take out passes. These were ordinary women — mothers, daughters,
grandmothers. Domestic workers came to march on their days off, those who
worked in industry took time off, and those who usually stayed home to care for
small children also came, bringing their children with them. They were united in
their determination to resist.

Ida Moretsele was not a political person. The mother of a two-year-old
daughter, Rebecca, she joined her neighbors to march to the native commissioner's offices on a warm day in October 1958. Rebecca slept on her mother's back
as Ida stood with hundreds of other women milling peacefully around the offices.
They refused to carry passes and demanded to be arrested. A group of police,
waving batons, none too gently took the women into custody and carted them off
to jail. Squashed into cells, there was barely room to stand, let alone sit. The
cement floors were filthy, and in the heat the smell of sweat and urine permeated

the air. There was no food or water, and Rebecca began to cry, as did other small children. Gently, Ida breast-fed her daughter, but her milk was almost gone, and soon Rebecca cried again. Softly, Ida sang to her daughter; the other women also hummed lullabies, and the babies slept in this dark hole of hell.

Wrote Maggie Resha, wife of leader Robert Resha, in her book *My Life in the Struggle*, published by the Congress of South African Writers in 1992:

> When you are in the struggle, you never really think that you are doing anything extraordinary, but simply that you are working side by side with your comrades-in-arms for the realisation of those ideals dear to you — freedom, justice and equality for all South Africans. . . . Women were fighting against the Pass Laws because of instinctive self protection from insecurity, self degradation and humiliation, which was epitomised by these laws. And from what they had experienced as mothers, wives and sweethearts of passbearers, they were fighting to protect their families from being plunged into disarray. Last, but not least, they were fighting to protect their children from being turned into the street — wandering, hungry orphans when both parents were picked up and locked in jail or sold to white farmers for slave labour.

In 1958, the ANC mounted a women's campaign calling upon women to demonstrate against the carrying of passes. Each woman was asked to come to the Johannesburg City Hall with a letter of protest addressed to the mayor of Johannesburg calling upon him not to cooperate with the issuing of passes to African women. Four thousand women arrived at the City Hall steps to protest. In twos and threes they came, so as not to constitute a gathering, which would have been illegal, but they came nonetheless. As usual, there was a police baton charge, and also, as usual, the women's protests were registered. And ignored.

Throughout 1958, women in Johannesburg protested against pass laws. The demonstrations were without exception nonviolent. Often they took the form of passive resistance, with the women presenting themselves at police stations and demanding to be arrested because they were not prepared to take the pass or *dompas* (from the Afrikaans word meaning "dumb pass") as it was called.

The protests culminated in a march of thirty-five hundred women through the streets of the city. It was a typical protest in that it was good-natured, with the women smiling and singing, and the atmosphere was almost jovial. Well-known African poet Don Mattera described such protesters as "Humour and anger marching side-by-side."

The women proceeded with dignity. When harassed by the police or jeered at by unsympathetic white onlookers, they ignored the heckling and continued undaunted. They were marching past the Johannesburg Magistrate's Court when suddenly and unexpectedly the police mounted a brutal baton charge. They lifted their sticks and began hitting the women, chasing them down the street. Several hundred women were arrested and loaded into *kwela-kwelas*, the police pickup vans, and driven off to jail. They appeared in court the following day on charges ranging from taking part in an illegal procession to disturbing the peace.

Finally, in 1963, after seven bitter years of antipass campaigning, which culminated in pass-burning throughout the country, the reference book system was installed, and African women, in order to acquire employment, were forced to take passes. These passes, which could only be issued by the native commissioner, contained personal information about the holder, including the date and place of birth. This determined where the holder could work and live, for there was no freedom of movement for blacks. Under influx control, any movement to another area — for employment or any other reason — required special permission and stamped approval in the reference book. If found in an area without permission, arrest, imprisonment or a fine, and then endorsement out were immediate.

In 1961, when the protests were increasing, the government passed the Unlawful Organisations Act, banning all liberation organizations, including the ANC and the PAC. A state of emergency was declared, under which thousands of people were detained without trial.

Along with the pass defiance campaigns, women were organizing on other fronts. In the townships of Durban, Natal, for example, brewing beer was a popular home industry — for some black women their sole means of support. The Durban Corporation, however, banned this activity, seeing it as competition to the government-run beer halls that the men were encouraged to frequent. The women, simultaneously being deprived of their own livelihood and seeing their men drinking away their money — which, ironically, went to implement the government legislation that oppressed them — decided to act. Florence Mkhize, ANCWL activist and organizer in Natal, was there on the day the women stormed the beer halls.

"Under the leadership of Dorothy Nyembe, we decided to fight this question of liquor. We knew the beer halls would cause misery in our homes. . . .

"We went to the beer halls to demonstrate against the men who were inside drinking. Mr. Bowan, the administrative manager from Durban, came to address us at Leho and he was accompanied by hundreds of policemen. He spoke, then gave us five minutes to disperse. The police began shooting at the women and one man died and one woman was injured. We were so angry that we became tigresses. We went into that beer hall and destroyed everything. Inside we were chasing the men and the police were chasing us. We were in the middle. We took the liquor tins and beat the men up."

The result of the women's demonstrations was an avoidance of the beer halls by the men for several months. "Our men became more responsible after that campaign." A second result of the campaign was that township women were given permission to brew four gallons of beer, which they could then sell.

The pressure to reject civil disobedience and take up arms had begun. This shift would be fueled by the brutal events of the coming decades, transforming the confrontation for men and women alike.

In 1955, the government initiated the notorious "Western Areas Removals Scheme" by which Sophiatown, a black area, was to be cleared for white development. Residents vowed to fight rather than move. In 1956, the ANC held a meeting in Freedom Square to protest against these forced removals. The leaders' deputations and the residents' protests were in vain. Sophiatown was bulldozed and cleared of blacks. The white suburb of Triomf (the Afrikaans word for *triumph*) was built in its place.

During the Sophia-town forced removals, one day in 1956 this woman returned from work to find her home demolished.

Ruth Mamphati, a courageous and fiery speaker, addressed a meeting at Freedom Square in Sophiatown in 1955 at the beginning of the removals.

Fund-raising for the ANC was always a problem. June Chabaku collects money to be used for the defense of those imprisoned and the transport of their relatives to and from jail. Although the ANC was unstructured during this time, people gave what they could to the cause.

OPPOSITE, TOP: On October 21, 1955, the women of Sophiatown marched on the native commissioner's office to protest against having to carry passes. Two hundred and forty-nine women were arrested by the police for holding an illegal procession. Hundreds of other women then rallied to support their imprisoned sisters, and by the end of the day, 584 women had been arrested.

OPPOSITE, BOTTOM: On April 5, 1959, at a meeting held at the Orlando East communal hall, a militant breakaway group from the ANC formed the Pan-Africanist Congress (PAC) under the leadership of Robert Sobukwe. These women emerged from the meeting and angrily threatened a security policeman, Mr. Sharp, who had been snooping around.

No event united the women of South Africa as did the passing of the legislation enforcing black women to carry pass books. The Federation of South African Women (FSAW) organized a massive countrywide women's protest. This was the triumphant moment, when on August 9, 1956, twenty thousand women marched on the Union Buildings, Pretoria, the seat of government, to protest against the carrying of passes. Sophie Williams, Rahima Moosa, Helen Joseph, and Lilian Ngoyi lead the women.

Three of the four leaders of the anti–pass book protest — Lilian Ngoyi, Helen Joseph, and Sophie Williams — attempt to present signed petitions opposing the legislation to Prime Minister J. G. Strijdom, who had fled the building. The women left their messages outside his office, but nevertheless, the security police removed them before Strijdom returned. Afterward, the women stood in silence for half an hour before triumphantly singing *Nkosi Sikeleli Afrika* (God Bless Africa).

"Strijdom, you have tampered with the women, you have struck a rock." These are the now-famous words of a protest song sung on this day to commemorate the historical march. The pacifist protest was memorable for its dignity.

In December 1956, a large number of anti-government protesters, including many leaders, were arrested by police. They appeared in court and were charged with treason against the state. Thus began the infamous Treason Trial, which dragged on for five years. Of 156 people of all races originally arrested, only thirty were eventually charged with plotting to overthrow the government. The state was never able to prove its case, and in March 1961, all were released. Here, activist June Chabaku hands out pamphlets to supporters.

Ruth First, journalist, activist, and member of the South African Communist Party, was one of twenty women arrested on charges of treason in 1956. On August 17, 1982, while working as a researcher at the Eduardo Mondlane University in Maputo, Mozambique, she was killed by a letter bomb. It was widely suspected that agents of the South African government planted the bomb.

A crowd outside the Johannesburg Drill Hall,
where the 1956 Treason Trial was held.

GEEN TOEGANG
NO ENTRY

54

Lilian Ngoyi, national president of the African National Congress Women's League and the Federation of South African Women, was an indefatigable fighter. Outspoken in her defiance of apartheid, she organized mass action on behalf of the antipass campaign. In 1961, she was banned and confined to the township of Mzimhlope for five years. An accused in the Treason Trial, she is seen here during a court break.

LEFT: Annie Silinga of the Federation of South African Women gestures defiantly during the Treason Trial in December 1956. Until the day she died, Silinga refused to carry a pass, thus forfeiting her right to an old-age pension.

These twins arrived to see their mother, who had been charged with treason. As she was brought into court, she caught a momentary glimpse of her children, intended to reassure her that all was well at home. While her husband worked, friends rallied around to care for the babies.

This was the traditional ANC freedom gesture, which was later banned — a clenched fist with raised thumb, then came the shout "*Amandla*" (power), then "*Ngawetu*" (it is ours). In 1956, these women gathered outside the Johannesburg Drill Hall, the scene of the Treason Trial, to offer support to their arrested leaders.

In 1958, thirty-five hundred women marched on Johannesburg to protest against the carrying of passes. Women from every walk of life came to march although they could lose their jobs. During the antipass march, the atmosphere was defiant but good-natured, and the protest was neither militant nor aggressive.

OVERLEAF: Antipass demonstrators were always harassed by the police. Here, some protesters argue back.

During the 1958 pass protest in Johannesburg, hundreds of women were apprehended and thrown into police vans.

After the march and the arrests, women marched again upon the Johannesburg Magistrate's Court in support of their colleagues who had been locked up. Suddenly the police mounted a baton charge. Lifting their sticks, they attacked the women, chasing them down the street.

Peter Magubane was arrested for photographing the charge in front of the court. Fellow photographer Jurgen Schadeberg recorded the moment. Magubane was later released, but not before his film had been removed from his camera.

In 1956, there was a series of bus boycotts to protest against the increase in fares, and everyone walked long distances rather than use buses. The boycotts started in Evaton and continued in Alexandra township for over a year. Almost twenty years later, in 1975, in Newcastle, Natal, people once again boycotted buses for the same reason. Here people walk from Emadadeni resettlement area to the town of Newcastle. They left before dawn to get to work and returned home long after sunset.

In the 1950s, this grandmother received the news that her grandson, Boy Sevenpence, was to be hanged. A notorious gangster, he'd robbed, assaulted, and killed township dwellers. Arrested by the police, he was found guilty and sentenced to death.

Veteran political campaigner Helen Joseph
was banned and placed under house arrest
on October 31, 1962. For nine years she
was confined to her house at night and during weekends and was allowed no visitors.
For over forty years, Joseph defied apartheid, in the process making many enemies.
Here, in 1978, she peers through her bed-
room window, which had been shattered by
an unknown assailant. As secretary of the
Federation of South African Women, a listed
Communist, and a defendant in the Treason
Trial, Joseph was detained, shot at, and
threatened many times over the years.

1960s: Sharpeville Massacre and the Increasing Role of Women of All Races in the Struggle

The sun was high in the sky on March 21, 1960, when hundreds of unarmed antipass protesters stood silently outside the police station in Sharpeville, a black township near Vereeniging in the Transvaal.

The demonstrators had refused to carry passes and, in an act of passive resistance, presented themselves to the police for arrest. Suddenly, the police opened fire on the group, and within forty seconds, sixty-nine people lay dead in the dry high-veld dust. Bodies were scattered on the earth, limbs were torn off or hanging by threads of skin, and there was blood everywhere. When the shooting began, those who stopped to help relatives or friends found themselves in the direct line of fire.

Innocent people attending a quiet protest were massacred, and many of them were shot in the back while running from the police. In his book *Shooting at Sharpeville*, Bishop Ambrose Reeves wrote: "So 216 families and over 500 children are paying the dreadful price of 40 seconds of uncontrollable firing at Sharpeville. The toll of irresponsibility finds its expression in amputations . . . wives left widows and children fatherless."

The shootings at Sharpeville caused waves of outrage around the world. In South Africa, the official reaction was predictable. The authorities immediately clamped down on the liberation movements, and bannings, detentions, and arrests escalated. Leaders throughout the country were imprisoned as the government crackdown increased. A state of emergency was proclaimed, and leaders were arrested.

A year later, South Africa left the Commonwealth and became a Republic. Meanwhile, the ANC had been forced underground, banned by the state in April 1960, as had been the Pan-Africanist Congress, a more militant group that, under the leadership of Robert Sobukwe, had broken from the ANC in April 1959 over the issue of the use of violence. Now, for the first time since its inception, the ANC itself was abandoning its policy of using passive resistance exclusively and made the momentous decision to use violence as an alternative. However, the ANC was committed to actions that avoided the loss of human life. Targets instead were government or police buildings or strategic installations.

The massacre at Sharpeville baptized the 1960s in blood. Not only did it further push the resistance organizations toward violent retaliation, it triggered a sweeping government crackdown. During the years that followed, new laws abounded in the effort to crush anti-apartheid opposition. The Unlawful Organisations Act of 1960, the Defence Act, the Police Amendment Act, the General Laws Amendment Act of 1961, then the General Laws Amendment Act of 1962, which became known as the Sabotage Act, all aided the state in viciously restraining anti-apartheid opposition. Sabotage was equated to treason and carried the death sentence. In 1962, Nelson Mandela, underground leader of the liberation movement, was arrested on charges of inciting workers and leaving the country illegally. His arrest, and those of other leaders, caused shock waves among the movements, especially in the short term. But there was a grass-roots resilience among the people, and they continued the struggle, albeit clandestinely.

The women's groups received the same treatment that their men were subjected to. The Federation of South African Women was particularly hard hit when most of its leaders and, indeed, many of its supporters were banned or imprisoned.

February 1, 1963, was a sad day, for on that day it became compulsory for all African women to carry pass books. Those who did not became instant nonbeings in the eyes of the state. They were not eligible for employment and could not claim pensions. White, Indian, and colored women were required by law to carry identity books. However, they were used strictly as a means of identification, not as a way of controlling the movement of people, as with Africans, for whom a correct stamp in a pass book often meant the difference between life and death.

Shortly after, the FSAW disbanded. The members of that brave organization had fought wholeheartedly and courageously for justice, dignity, and freedom from oppression. They had been hounded by the police and the security branch, their phones had been tapped, they had been raided in the early hours of the morning and dragged off to police cells for questioning. For many members, it had been almost impossible to live a normal life because of police and state harassment. Today, more than thirty years later, the ideals and objectives of the Federation of South African Women still burn fiercely in the hearts of women.

The 1960s were a time of repression and hardship for women, as the apartheid machinery ground relentlessly on. Political activists spent more time in prison than out, and if not incarcerated, they were banned or placed under house arrest, an extrajudicial form of restriction no less evil than jail for anyone innocent of a crime.

The policy of relocation begun in the 1950s under the Group Areas Act expanded. In order to clear the land for white settlement, blacks were forcibly removed from where they had lived and farmed all their lives. Urban blacks were moved to far, inconvenient outlying areas with few facilities. When the established suburb of District Six in Cape Town was cleared and bulldozed to make way for whites, the coloreds, Indians, and Africans who had lived there were moved to localities on the desolate Cape Flats. Squatter camps sprung up as displaced and desperate people tried unsuccessfully to put down roots.

It was unabashed government policy that blacks give way to whites, and this was enforced in all fields. There was job reservation in the workplace, with skilled jobs going to whites, menial jobs to blacks. White teachers received more pay than their black counterparts; white doctors received more pay than their black colleagues. Blacks were discriminated against in every facet of life.

Agnes Miya was born in a small village near Mqanduli in the Transkei. She lived with her family in a hut on a rolling green hill, an unbelievably beautiful part of South Africa. But the beauty was superficial. The children of the area had swollen bellies and runny noses because of malnutrition, and more often than not, the crops withered and died because of drought or disease. In the village where Agnes lived, there were only women, children, and a few grandfathers too old to work, for the men were away working. They would be gone for years, and sometimes they never came back. Agnes Miya traveled to Cape Town to find a job that would enable her to send money home to her younger brothers and sisters.

She settled in the squatter camp of Crossroads, found work as a cleaner, and formed a relationship with a young man from a neighboring village. After a few years, they had a baby daughter. Because Crossroads was an unofficial squatter camp, temporary in the eyes of the government, its inhabitants were relentlessly plagued by the authorities, who brought in bulldozers to demolish the humble tin and cardboard shacks. Agnes Miya hired a young fourteen-year-old girl to care for her daughter while she worked. One day, she returned to find her shack flattened and her baby missing. For hours she searched in vain for her child among the corrugated iron sheets and other debris. Heartbroken, she thought her daughter had died. Three days later, she discovered by chance that her baby and the young girl had been picked up in a police raid and endorsed back to the Transkei.

Two weeks later, after investigation and help from the Black Sash and church organizations, Agnes was reunited with her baby. She was lucky; many women in similar circumstances never found their young children.

Agnes and her husband returned to Crossroads, built another shack, and resumed their lives. They had no choice, because to return to the Transkei would have meant certain starvation. Whenever camps were cleared by officials, women resisted by standing in front of the bulldozers and refusing to make way. They were often arrested and their homes destroyed.

SHACK DWELLERS

Aiming so high

But reaching the top

of corrugated iron roofs.

Every day it's the same:

Hoping the bulldozers don't come

To raze down my den.

Every day is one hope:

Hoping the criminals don't come

To steal my pretty furniture.

Every day is grief:

Hoping the chicocos don't come

To confiscate my last clothes.

Every night the same dream:

Hoping the township managers

Will wake up with some humanity tomorrow.

Every day the same vision:

Hoping for some change in the system

Which oppresses the poor.

MHLANGANISI NGONYAMA

To get rid of troublemakers, the state devised the system of banishment. Under the Native Administration Act of 1927 and its later amendments, those who opposed the government too vociferously, or those who were successful in gathering antigovernment support, were often physically removed from their familiar environment — their homes, families, and jobs — and banished to remote areas. It was an effective way of silencing opponents because often those banished were placed among different tribes with whom they were unable to communicate. For example, a Xhosa-speaking person might be banished to a Sesotho-speaking area. In the wilderness, some people disappeared; others barely subsisted, and sometimes they starved to death.

It was women who disclosed the brutality of banishment to the world media. Tireless fighters and activists Helen Joseph and Amina Cachalia traveled the length and breadth of South Africa seeking out those who had been banished. Their aim was first to ensure they were still alive, then second to draw the attention of the civilized world to their plight.

Amina Cachalia of the South African Indian Congress served her first sentence in 1952, one of the first Indian women to go to jail. Active in the SAFW, she was also a member of the Human Rights Welfare Committee for the Banished. In the 1960s, she was banned, along with her husband, Yusuf, a well-known Indian Congress leader, who was placed under house arrest.

Said Helen Joseph of her and Amina's experiences: "We exposed the horrors of the system, the agony of the banished."

On May 1, 1963, there was an amendment to the General Laws Amendment Act of 1961, and this amendment became known as the Sabotage Act. A year later, at the Rivonia trial, on June 12, 1964, eight men — six Africans, one white, and one Indian — were sentenced to life imprisonment on Robben Island. They were charged with committing 199 acts of sabotage and planning to overthrow the state. Sentenced were Nelson Mandela (already in jail since 1962), Walter Sisulu, Dennis Goldberg, Govan Mbeki, Ahmed Kathadra, Raymond Mhlaba, Elias Matsoaledi, and Andrew Mlangeni. Most of the men served well over twenty years; the longest serving was Nelson Mandela, who was only released after he had been in prison for twenty-seven years.

Apartheid and all its vicious tentacles permeated everyone's life. Under the Immorality Act, to love someone of a different color was a criminal offense punishable by a jail sentence. Police sordidly and stealthily spied on couples who dared to love across the color bar. If caught in the act, they were prosecuted; if found guilty, jailed. Countless people committed suicide rather than go to prison.

Under the Population Registration Act, one of the cornerstones of apartheid, government officials often classified newborn babies of doubtful parentage by using the "pencil test," in which a pencil would be placed in the child's curls. If the pencil stuck (because the hair was frizzy), the baby was classified as colored, which relegated the child to second-class citizenship and a lifetime of hardship and deprivation.

Families were torn apart by this shameful law. One of the most heartbreaking cases was that of Sandra Laing, a fresh-faced youngster of twelve who lived in the eastern Transvaal. Her parents and brothers were white, as was she. But her skin was darkish, her hair tightly curled, and her nose small and flattish.

Parents of children where she attended school with her brothers complained to the authorities about the darkness of her skin. They objected, they said, to their children being in the same school as a *kaffir* (a derogatory term for an African). Sandra was removed from school, reclassified as colored, and ostracized by everyone, including her parents. Her father actually disowned her.

The 1950s and 1960s saw the emergence of many leading women in the struggle. Winnie Mandela, the first African social worker in South Africa, was twenty-four when she married ANC leader Nelson Mandela in 1958. An activist, she was banned under the Supression of Communism Act from 1962 to 1975. Not only Communists were banned under this act. During this period, virtually all anti-government activists were branded "Communists." This included churchmen and many others far to the right of communism.

Winnie Mandela, always defiant, refused to heed her restrictions and was twice charged for contravening her banning order in 1967. With her husband serving a life sentence on Robben Island, she, like countless other women in the struggle, had to be both mother and father to her two small daughters. Detained under Section 6 of the Terrorism Act in 1969, she was held in solitary confinement for seventeen months. Friends and family cared for her children. In 1970, she was acquitted, then banned again and placed under house arrest. Throughout perpetual government harassment, she stayed at the forefront in the struggle for majority rule. Her support for those involved in fighting repression was visible. With her husband, more than any other person she became the symbol of the struggle. A thorn in the flesh of the government, she was charged on numerous occasions for disregarding her banning orders.

She received a new banning order in 1976, and the following year was banished to the godforsaken town of Brandfort in the Orange Free State. There she lived with her daughter Zinzi, on the outskirts in the dusty black township section, Phatakahle, in a small, austere house with three tiny rooms, no ceilings, and an outside toilet at the end of the backyard. Outside, too, was the only running water, a cold water tap, which often, on winter mornings, was frozen solid.

The township dwellers were forbidden to communicate with the young wife of Nelson Mandela. She and they disregarded the order, and within weeks Winnie Mandela had organized a form of resistance to racist oppression in the white town of Brandfort, where, in the local stores, blacks were prohibited from using the same entrance as whites. Winnie Mandela ignored the "whites only" signs and used the whites' entrances. The township people followed her example and have done so ever since.

In 1986, Winnie Mandela was interviewed by journalist and author Beata Lipman for the book *We Make Freedom*. Describing detention, Winnie Mandela said:

> Detention means that midnight knock when all about you is quiet. It means those blinding torches shone simultaneously through every window of your house before the door is kicked open. It means seizure at dawn, dragged away from little children screaming and clinging to your skirt, imploring the man dragging mummy to leave her alone. It means, as it was for me, being held in a single cell with the light burning twenty four hours so that I lost track of time and was unable to tell whether it was day or night.
>
> Every single moment of your life is regulated and supervised. Complete isolation from the outside world, no privacy, no visitor, lawyer or minister. It means no one to talk to each twenty-four hours, no knowledge of how long you will be imprisoned and why you are imprisoned, getting medical attention from the doctor only when you are seriously ill.
>
> The emptiness of those hours of solitude is unbearable. Your company is your solitude, your blanket, your mat, your sanitary bucket, your mug and yourself.
>
> All this in preparation for the inevitable hell — interrogation. It is meant to crush your individuality completely, to change you into a docile being from whom no resistence can arise, to terrorise you, to intimidate you into silence.

Winnie Mandela has always been a figure of controversy. Fiery and militant, she is fiercely loved or fiercely hated. Helen Joseph describes her feelings toward

Winnie in her autobiography, *Side by Side:* "When I recall the riches of togetherness, then I realise how privileged I have been to have the affection of this woman who has transcended the hardships and persecutions heaped upon her almost beyond human endurance. She has emerged from it all as indestructable." Today, Helen Joseph still regards Winnie Mandela as one of her closest friends, a woman who has suffered more than most. "When I see her," she says, "I want to put my arms around her and give her a hug."

In 1986, Winnie Mandela was interviewed on radio. Asked how apartheid had affected her, she said: "I am terribly brutalized inside. I know my soul is scarred. I know I am bleeding inside all the time. I know the pain of my people's suffering, the pain of having a husband behind bars for twenty-five years, the pain of bringing up children under the atmosphere I've brought them up in is so great inside. But what has happened has not brutalized me to the extent of being consumed in hate. If I had been, I think I wouldn't have been able to see the following day.

"It is because of the hope that exudes inside one, that today's suffering is for a better tomorrow."

Winnie Mandela's relationship with the ANC and the United Democratic Front (UDF) has, in past years, been strained. The relationship with the ANC gradually improved after the release of her husband from Robben Island, and for a while, she took her place beside him in the social and political context. However, her involvement in the circumstances surrounding the death of fourteen-year-old Stompie Moeketsi Seipei in 1989, and the resultant court case in 1991, brought her negative international news coverage and exacerbated the strain with the ANC.

In the mid-1980s, Winnie Mandela became closely associated with a group of youths known as the Mandela United Football Club. Regarded as her bodyguards, the "football club" was viewed with fear by the people of Soweto, where, it is said, they exercised a reign of terror. Stompie Moeketsi Seipei and three other boys were taken against their will by members of the football club to the Mandela household, where they were beaten. Stompie's body was later discovered in the veld. Jerry Richardson, the coach of the Mandela United Football Club, was convicted of the murder of Stompie.

Found guilty of the kidnapping and assault of the four youths, Winnie Mandela was sentenced to six years imprisonment. The case is presently on appeal and she is out on bail.

On April 14, 1992, the Mandelas announced that they would separate. In a moving press statement announcing the separation, Nelson Mandela said: "... She endured the persecutions heaped upon her by the government and never wavered from her commitment to the struggle for freedom.... My love for her (Nomzana Winnie Mandela) remains undiminished.... I shall personally never regret the life Comrade Nomzana and I tried to share together. Circumstances beyond our control, however, dictated that it should be otherwise. I part from my wife with no recriminations. I embrace with all the love and affection I have nursed for her inside and outside prison from the moment I first met her."

In the 1960s, the role of women in the struggle increased. As before, they resisted forced removals and mass evictions, but the scope of their protests expanded. For the first time, domestic workers objected to their terms of employment, their poor salaries, the fact that while caring lovingly for their white charges, they could not see their own children for months and even years on end. Domestic service is probably the largest single type of work for black women in South Africa, and these workers (along with farm laborers) are among the most exploited. The relationship between employer and domestic worker has always been paternalistic, and until fairly recently domestic workers were treated almost as slaves, virtually without rights. Today there is a domestic workers union that attempts to safeguard the interest of workers, and wages have increased minimally, in part as a result of articles in the media about the hardships domestics suffer. Still, their lives are filled with anguish, as shown in this poem by a young worker:

DOMESTIC WORKERS

We are called girls

We are called maids

It is as if we are small

It is as if we are children

We are told what to do

We are told what to say

We are told what to think

We are told what to wear

We are women

We are mothers

Too much work can break our bodies

Too much suffering can break our hearts

Our problem is that we live alone

Our problem is that we work alone

Our problem is that we suffer alone

Our problem is that we are paid so little

GRACE TINY SITHEBE

During the decade, women became even more active in trade unions, in the workplace. And, as always, they were united in their cause — the fight against apartheid and oppression. Again, prisons filled to overflowing with pass offenders, and in the hundreds of thousands, women spent long nights on icy cement floors. When carried away in *kwela-kwelas*, they would sing and raise their fists in the ANC freedom salute.

Such is the nature of the black women in South Africa.

I WANT TO BE FREE

I want to tear away the rugged walls

I want to run through the city

Run until I reach the rolling hills

I want to run and dance wildly

I want to stroke the red earth

With my bare hands

I want to lie naked like a lizard

Under the hot African sun

I want to be free

JULIA CUMES

There were many whites who joined them, in spirit if not in suffering. And there were many whites who suffered, too — by being detained, banned, and placed under house arrest. There were the women of the Black Sash, who ceaselessly campaigned for human rights, and there was Helen Suzman, valiant and fearless, who was, for so many years the sole opposition member of Parliament, the only voice to champion the cause of those who were voiceless. A fearless debater, she was well respected even by her enemies in the government. She was the only contact between many political prisoners and their families.

When Suzman gave up her seat in Parliament in 1989, she was the longest-serving member of Parliament. For thirty-six years, she vigorously opposed apartheid and represented the values of liberalism.

Helen Suzman's lifelong efforts again demonstrate how the fight to combat apartheid in South Africa brought together women of conviction and strength from all races and all walks of life.

This is a nonperson who officially does not
exist. Homeless and destitute, too old to
work, she has no family or income. Because
she has never been registered, she has no
reference book and thus is unable to qualify
for a pension. Living in an abandoned car,
she is cared for and fed by people in the
vicinity, many of whom can barely support
themselves.

ABOVE: In 1967, blacks were forbidden to move freely around South Africa or live where they wished unless they had the correct documentation. Women came to the cities, either to live illegally with their migrant-laborer husbands or to seek work. If caught in an area without permission to be there, they were arrested, charged, jailed, then endorsed out and sent home. These women are being repatriated from Alexandra township.

RIGHT: Forced removals caused hardship. People without passes, jobs, or houses eked out an existence wherever they could. Illegal squatter camps sprang up everywhere. These were only temporary, for regularly government authorities demolished the settlements. At Modderdam, Cape Town, in 1978, these women try to salvage their belongings as their homes are bulldozed.

OPPOSITE: In 1962, Pimville was one of the oldest and most lively squatter townships on the Highveld, and people came from all over South Africa to settle here, though the conditions were abominable. Shacks like the one above would catch fire and be totally gutted within seconds. Left homeless, this mother and her four children were lucky to escape with their lives.

78

In 1967, these people were forcibly removed from their farms and villages to the bleak resettlement area of Limehill, Natal. Within weeks, the barren land had claimed its first victim, a ten-year-old child who died of starvation. This is the child's funeral.

On March 21, 1960, protesters refusing to carry pass books stood silently outside the Sharpeville police station and, in defiance, presented themselves for arrest. Unexpectedly, the police opened fire on the unarmed protesters and within seconds, sixty-nine people died and one hundred eighty-six were wounded. Here, a victim is placed in a police van by black policemen, whose sympathy often lay with the protesters.

TOP: Young and old, men and women were mowed down by the barrage of bullets. Those who stopped to help their relatives or friends put themselves in danger. Here, an injured woman is carried away.

BOTTOM: A mass funeral was held for the Sharpeville victims. Families and friends wept as their loved ones were laid to rest.

At the graveside,
members of the PAC
held their banner while
waiting for the funeral
service to start.

RIGHT: The Sharpeville
funeral.

Pass legislation was the greatest single cause
of protest among women in South Africa.
Here, in Shantytown in 1961, these men
and women defiantly burn their passes in
protest.

CRY, THE BELO VED COUNTRY.

ABOVE: In May 1962, the minister of justice, B. J. Vorster, piloted a general law amendment bill through Parliament, which established a new offense — sabotage — and also gave certain government ministers power above the rule of law; thus, the government was no longer bound by law. A protest outside the Johannesburg Supreme Court against this act is broken up by the police.

LEFT: During demonstrations against the Sabotage Bill, a stinkbomb was hurled at the demonstrators. This woman flees down the steps of the Johannesburg City Hall.

OVERLEAF: In 1964, during the Rivonia trial, several leaders were arrested and charged with high treason. Eight of them received life sentences, including Nelson Mandela, Walter Sisulu, and Govan Mbeki. Daily, these women stood outside the court protesting against the trial and demanding the release of their leaders.

Winnie Mandela, banished and placed under house arrest, was restricted to her three-room house in Orlando West, Soweto, from 6 P.M. to 6 A.M. Allowed no visitors other than her children, she had to report weekly to the police. The police harassed her day and night, raiding her house, taking her away for questioning. Nevertheless, she vigorously supported the banned ANC and organized secret meetings. Her clandestine antigovernment activities led to her arrest, and she was charged with twenty-one other people under the Terrorism Act in 1969. Here, she peers through her gate.

Soweto, the sprawling black township four-
teen miles from Johannesburg, is home to
at least three million blacks. Most people
commute by bus, train, or mini taxi, and
because of the sheer volume of traffic,
accidents are common. In 1967, a train
crashed in the main Soweto line and several
people were killed, including this woman's
husband. At the funeral service in Ntlazane,
she weeps for her man who left for work
and never returned.

Forcibly removed from Vrededorp, this Indian mother settled with her family in Lover's Walk, Mayfair. The police, acting on a complaint from white neighbors who objected to having Indians living in their midst, evicted her from her home. In defiance, she returned, and again they evicted her. This scene was enacted several times as this proud woman kept returning to her home. Eventually she and her family were forced to squat, homeless, in the street.

The Naidoo family of Doornfontein, Johannesburg, has always been prominent in the struggle and they have been active supporters of the ANC, especially during the years the organization was banned. Ramani Dinath tearfully bids farewell to her elderly mother, Amma Naidoo, as she leaves to join her husband in exile in London. Her sister, Shanti, and brothers, Prema and Indris, were both detained; Indris served a jail sentence on Robben Island.

Mrs. Nokukhanya Luthuli, wife of Nobel Peace Prize–winner Chief Albert Luthuli, former president of the ANC, attends her husband's funeral in Groutville, Natal, in 1967. The verdict at the inquest of this great leader's death — that he had been "struck by a train" — was never accepted by the Luthuli family.

1970s–Present: June 16, 1976 Uprising through the Abolition of Apartheid and the Future of South Africa

In the 1970s, a single event dramatically intensified the anti-apartheid movement. At this critical moment, the women of South Africa played a supporting role. It was their children who stepped forth — in the explosive June 16, 1976 Soweto uprising. This confrontation marked the beginning of the change in South Africa. From this time on, the youngest generation of black South Africans embraced the Black Consciousness movement and became increasingly politicized. The issue that sparked the Soweto uprising, and brought the country to this irrevocable turning point, was education.

Black education in South Africa has always been a festering sore. For years, black parents have been dissatisfied by the poor quality of education received by their children. In 1976, as today, education was compulsory for white children but not for blacks. And like everything else in South Africa, education was segregated. There were white, Indian, colored, Chinese, and African schools. The last fell under the Department of Bantu Education, and the entire system was — and still is — grossly inferior to the others.

The Bantu Education Bill was piloted through Parliament in 1953 by Dr. Hendrik Verwoerd, minister of native affairs. On June 7, 1954, Dr. Verwoerd made a lengthy parliamentary policy speech on Bantu Education. He said: "The economic structure of our country, of course, results in the Natives in large numbers having to earn their living in the service of Europeans. For that reason it is essential that Bantu students should receive instruction in both official languages (English and Afrikaans) from the beginning so that they can even in the lower primary school develop an ability to speak and understand them. . . ." It was clear that Bantu education was designed to keep blacks subservient to whites.

African children themselves were frustrated and bitter; they wanted a first-class education, the same as white children received. In the mid-1970s, this frustration and anger grew. Amid the rumbling in the townships, the Afrikaans-speaking government decided to implement Afrikaans intead of English as the medium of instruction in African schools. To African children, Afrikaans was seen as the language of the oppressor. This was the final match that lit the bonfire of resentment against apartheid that erupted into the June 16 uprising.

On June 16, 1976, the children of Soweto high schools decided to march in protest against the use of Afrikaans. The intention was to hold a mass meeting to air their grievances. Thousands of students converged on Orlando West High School, some carrying placards that the police tried to remove. The situation was volatile. The police panicked and opened fire. Thirteen-year-old Hector Peterson was shot dead. And then the students' anger exploded. Rioting broke out and spread to other townships. Over six hundred people lost their lives in the ensuing violence that day and in the following weeks. People were arrested and imprisoned. But whereas in earlier years it had been the older people who had protested, now it was the youth. And girls became as militant and active as boys. They joined underground liberation movements, and several thousand left the country for training in guerrilla warfare, with the intention of returning to overthrow the apartheid regime.

The Black Consciousness movement is an umbrella term used to describe the Black Consciousness ideology and the many groups and organizations aligned to these ideals. Black Consciousness began in the 1960s, and in early days, it was supported mainly by students. In the mid-1970s, Steve Biko had become the articulate and active leader of the Black Consciousness movement. Stressing the need for black pride and autonomy, his message was perceived as a serious threat by the government.

On September 12, 1977, Biko died in detention. Maltreated, horribly injured, and chained to the wall by the security police, he was neglected for two days, then transported naked from Port Elizabeth to Pretoria, a twelve-hour journey, in the back of a police van. Unaccompanied by a doctor and critically ill, he died.

There was outrage at his death, both home and abroad. Biko's wife, Ntsiki, emerged as one of South Africa's unsung heroines, and is still today a role model for many South African women. Despite problems within her marriage, she had a touching devotion to her husband, and she sufferrd her loss with great dignity. Biko's close friend and associate, Dr. Mamphela Ramphele, bore him a son soon after his death; she named him Hlumelo — a Xhosa word meaning "spring from a new branch." Dr. Ramphele was banned and banished to Lenyenye, a remote area in the district of Tzaneen in the northeastern Transvaal. At the time of her banning, Dr. Ramphele was superintendent of the Zanempilo Clinic in King Williams Town, a clinic founded by the Black Community Programmes. An exile in Tzaneen, and under the most restrictive banning orders, she nevertheless established a clinic for the community.

Courageously, she repeatedly defied her banning orders so that she could tend to her patients. Today, Dr. Ramphele is the deputy vice-chancellor of the University of Cape Town and a research fellow in the department of social anthropology. The change in her status demonstrates the changing nature of a new South Africa. It also demonstrates the extraordinary caliber of this remarkable woman who could rise above severe hardship and repression.

The end of the 1970s and the early 1980s led to a consolidation of what had gone before. Although there was increasing political change, some things remained the same. As they do today.

In the rural areas, women and children still battle alone while their men, migrant laborers, live in cities for the greater part of the year. Squatter camps have multiplied, a situation exacerbated by drought in the rural areas, which has increased the flow of people to the urban areas to seek work.

Although the situation of domestic workers has nominally improved, the majority of them still live apart from their families, caring for white children while their own are brought up by relatives or friends in distant villages. They are away from their children for long periods and often return to find they are virtually strangers in their own homes.

The 1980s were marked by increased resistance to apartheid, as underground liberation movements accelerated their campaign against oppression. The use of violence by government and security forces on the one side and by underground opposition movements on the other escalated. These were the years of the armed struggle with women and children at the forefront. Sometimes they paid for their beliefs with their lives.

Over the years, the liberation movements armed their members, and quasi-military movements were formed. Shortly after the ANC and PAC were banned in 1960, ANC supporters formed Umkhonto we Sizwe (Spear of the Nation), while militant PAC members formed Poqo (an abbreviation of the Xhosa name UmAfrika Poqo, meaning "blacks only"). In 1968, the military wing of the PAC became known as the Azanian People's Liberation Army (APLA).

Violence in black townships has escalated and several reasons have been advanced as the cause of the violence and resultant bloodshed: apartheid, the ethnic divisions between black people, the political rivalry between the ANC and the Inkatha Freedom Party (predominantly Zulu speakers), the involvement of certain members of the security forces and a sinister "Third Force" suspected and proven to be members of the security forces.

Caught in the crossfire are countless innocent people. One was Sicelo Dhlomo, who was murdered in 1988.

Sicelo was eighteen years old; a student leader, he was featured in a CBS television documentary entitled "The Children of Apartheid" in late 1987. During the interview, Sicelo, a likable teenager with an engaging personality, gripped the attention of millions of viewers with graphic descriptions of life under apartheid.

On one occasion that year, while on his way to school, Sicelo had been picked up by the police and detained. The account of the incident by his mother, Sylvia Jele, was damning: "He was kicked and beaten all over his body before being released the same week." After another bout of detention, Sicelo stated: "I am going to fight for my people, my rights and for a democratic South Africa. I may have to die to achieve this."

After he'd been detained several times in 1987, Sylvia Jele spoke to a Washington tribunal about the effects of detention on children. She told of her experiences as a mother of an activist and the terrible fears she had for her son each time he was detained and harassed by the police. Unfortunately, the tribunal had no effect on the situation in South Africa.

It was not even a year later that Sylvia Jele's worst fears were realized and Sicelo lay dead. On January 26, 1988, his body was found near his house in Emdeni, Soweto. He had been shot through the head.

Around the time of his murder, Sicelo, when not busy with youth activities, worked voluntarily for the Detainees Parents Support Committee (DPSC), formed by a group of concerned parents to protest against their children's detention and to safeguard them against ill-treatment while in prison. Sicelo was described by his fellow workers as a brave young man, industrious, and with a mature political commitment. Said a colleague: "Sicelo was robbed of his youth and forced into adulthood by the political situation. In a short time he became everyone's friend, and we are devastated by his death."

The week before his death, the police called Sicelo in for questioning about his role in the DPSC and his other perceived antigovernment activities and what he had said in the CBS documentary.

His murder, along with those of several other well-known South African activists — including human-rights lawyer Victoria Mxenge, who was stabbed and shot by four unknown men — remains unsolved.

Like so many other South African mothers, Sylvia Jele made the greatest sacrifice that could be asked of a mother. Today, her resolve to continue is unquenched. "I am part of the struggle," she says.

With the rise of armed resistance by the people came clashes between them and the police, often resulting in townships and squatter camps resembling war zones, with broken and bloody bodies everywhere. "Necklacing," the gruesome and barbaric retribution by antigoverment supporters against suspected *impimpis* (police or government informers), increased. The victim, a car tire placed around his neck, would be doused in gasoline, then set alight, dying in agony. Shoot-outs between the police and armed civilians increased, and massacres occurred with depressing regularity. In recent years, several judicial commissions have been appointed to investigate such incidents.

The 1980s saw the emergence of extra-parliamentary politics, notably the formation in 1983 of the United Democratic Front, a united political resistance against the government, with more than six hundred affiliated organizations. The UDF's stated aim was to create a true democracy in which all South Africans could participate.

Although former President P. W. Botha spoke about change, it was only when President F. W. de Klerk came into power that the process of real reform was implemented. On February 2, 1990, President de Klerk unbanned all resistance movements; a week later, he released Nelson Mandela from prison.

Apartheid was officially abolished on February 1, 1991, when President de Klerk announced the proposed scrapping of repressive legislation — the Group Areas Act, the Population Registration Act, and the Land Act were repealed in one fell swoop.

Toward the end of 1990, the ANC Women's League was reestablished, and in May 1991, Gertrude Shope was elected the first president, with Albertina Sisulu as her vice-president.

Today, the political emphasis is firmly on negotiation and national reconciliation, which is why it is hard to understand the violence sweeping the country.

There has to be an understanding of South African history to appreciate that this violence is more than just a bloody clash between Zulu- and Xhosa-speaking people.

The system of apartheid has bred certain unfavorable socioeconomic circumstances for the majority of black people, who have been forced to live in ghettolike townships lacking in facilities.

The system of migrant labor has produced a large force of men and women who come to live in the townships adjoining the cities in single-sex hostels. The hostels are prisonlike and austere, and under these conditions, they become strongholds for particular groups.

The squatters, if anything, live under even more adverse conditions than the hostel dwellers, and daily there is the very real threat that their camps will be destroyed by the authorities. Squatters are threatened on so many fronts — by the police and the authorities who wish them cleared from the area, and by the hostel dwellers who might come from a different political and language group — that they are defensive, volatile communities.

Because black schooling has been seen as an instrument of apartheid under the National Party government, many black schools have been burned down by pupils as a protest against the system, or closed because of ongoing disruption and violence. It is often pointed out that almost a whole generation of young blacks has been denied education as a result. Gangs of uneducated, unemployed, and unemployable youths roam the townships, contributing to and perpetuating the circle of violence, crime, hardship, and more violence.

Because of the changing political scenario in South Africa, there is a power struggle between the key players — the ANC, the Inkatha Freedom Party, and the National Party — and it is not unreasonable to believe that violence is exploited by those who are unscrupulous. Added to this is the threat of terrorist violence from far-right-wing supporters, who warn of a "terrible revolution" when a majority government is installed.

Violence is not restricted to men — women are becoming increasingly more militant. However, Lloyd Vogelman, the director of the University of the Witwatersrand's Research Project on Violence, believes women become engaged in violence only as a desperate last resort. "Women feel that unless they destroy the enemy, their lives and those of their family would be seriously jeopardized," he says. He points out that, with traditional family structure broken down, women find themselves in the unaccustomed role of head of the household, with the added duties of protecting and defending, not a normal role for black women.

During township violence, women have marched aggressively, brandishing pitchforks, pangas, and other improvised weapons. "We are taking up spears and guns and moving into the front line against the enemy," said Black Housewives League vice-chairman Andronicah August in 1990. "It's our children who are being killed, our homes that are being burnt down, so even if we don't want to, we have to take sides and fight out of necessity. Giving emotional support to our husbands and sons is not enough any more."

Nineteen ninety-one was known as "The Year of the Massacres" because of the escalating violence in Johannesburg and surrounding townships on the East and West Rand and in the Vaal Triangle.

However, throughout the country there is a strong desire for peace and an end to the lawlessness and violence. On Easter Sunday, April 20, 1992, for the first time in South Africa's history, three leaders, President F. W. de Klerk, ANC President Nelson Mandela, and the president of the Inkatha Freedom Party, Chief Magosuthu Buthelezi, met at Moria to address over a million members of the Zion Christian Church in a plea for peace. The leaders unconditionally committed themselves to doing everything in their power to end violence and to move speedily toward a widely acceptable political settlement.

Among the majority of all the peoples of South Africa, there is a genuine and determined desire to see the establishment of a new peaceful and democratic order. But in a country plagued with such a turbulent recent past, the road to peace is a difficult one.

On June 17, 1992, a second Sharpeville shocked the world when forty innocent people were massacred at Boipatong, the tiny Vaal settlement near Vanderbijlpark to the south of Johannesburg.

In the dark of night, people living in the squatter camp of Boipatong were attacked as they were sleeping in their beds by a large group of men brandishing firearms and other weapons. They were shot, hacked, and chopped to pieces. Among those murdered were twenty-three women, including a mother and her eighteen-month-old son and a young woman nine months pregnant.

The attackers were alleged to have come from the KwaMadala hostel, an Inkatha stronghold. This was later verified by the police, who arrested several men from the hostel and charged them with murder. All those killed were regarded as ANC supporters. The police were accused of complicity and siding with those who mounted the attack. Witnesses stated before a judicial commission that police *casspirs* had broken down walls of the homes of the squatters to allow the Zulu-speaking attackers into the homes.

Debbie Yazbek, chief photographer of the *Sunday Star*, covered the Boipatong massacre for her paper. The memories of the twisted and maimed bodies she saw will haunt her forever.

Said Bishop Peter Storey at the mass funeral for the victims: "Something devilish happened at Boipatong. As your tears fall today, we weep with you." In a day of tragedy, one of the saddest sights was seeing a young mother and son buried together in the same grave.

Despite the terrible violence — in fact, because of it — the women of South Africa continue to fight for peace. Now, more than at any other time, their determination to end what Gertrude Shope, president of the ANC Women's League, calls "senseless violence" is strengthened.

Throughout the country, nonracial women's organizations such as the Federation of Transvaal Women (FedTRAW), the Natal Organisation of Women (NOW), and the Cape Town–based United Women's Congress (UWCO) are actively campaigning for an end to all discrimination, for equal rights, and, above all, for peace in the land. As Gertrude Shope says: "We have hope."

TOP RIGHT: After the flood, an Indian woman hangs up her identity book to dry. All whites, Indians, coloreds, and Chinese were required to carry identity books containing identity details.

BOTTOM RIGHT: A group of domestic workers looking at a newly issued pass book. Unlike the identity book required by other racial groups, African women had to carry a pass otherwise known as a reference book, which was stamped with permission to live and work in an area. Thousands of women were summarily arrested, jailed, and endorsed out of Johannesburg to the rural areas from the period 1956 to 1986, when the act was finally repealed. Apartheid laws made innocent people criminals.

OPPOSITE: During the Natal floods, homes, roads, and bridges were washed away. Those who lived in the black and Indian townships suffered most as their shacks were devastated by the raging waters. This young mother still counts herself lucky. Her children are alive. Patiently she stands in a soup queue.

These mourners were attending a funeral in Soweto for a victim shot by the police during the ongoing uprising, in 1978. They had just reached the gates of the Avalon Cemetery when they were teargassed by the police who tried to disperse the crowds, because large gatherings were not allowed. Actions like these inflamed young activists, and in future years the response to police and government aggression was increasing militancy.

These are some of the young schoolgirls who changed the course of history in South Africa when they rose in defiance of apartheid rule on June 16, 1976. Then, as now, education was compulsory only for whites, and black education was grossly inferior. In June, the Department of Bantu (African) Education decided to implement Afrikaans as the medium of instruction in black schools. Afrikaans was seen as the language of the oppressor, and the children protested against its use. Thousands marched to the Orlando West High School. An incident occurred, the police opened fire, and thirteen-year-old Hector Peterson was shot dead. This was the beginning of the June 16 uprising.

During the uprising on June 16, 1976, this Alexandra township mother found herself about to give birth in the midst of a riot situation. A sympathetic policeman placed her in an armored vehicle and escorted her to the hospital.

Hector Peterson, the first victim of the June 16 uprising to be shot dead, was picked up and carried by his sister. The moving photograph of her doing so made world headlines. Here, at her brother's funeral, she is comforted by members of the grieving family.

The impact of the
June 16 uprising
spread to neighboring
townships. On June 18,
in Alexandra town-
ship, the police opened
fire upon the crowd
and a bullet just
missed photographer
Peter Magubane's face
and instead hit this
girl in the stomach,
causing an ugly
wound. Many others
died.

OPPOSITE: During the
June 16 uprising, this
resident of Mofolo,
Soweto, lost her hus-
band when he was
gunned down by the
police. Unable to
come to terms with
her loss, she wept as
friends rallied round
to offer her comfort.

107

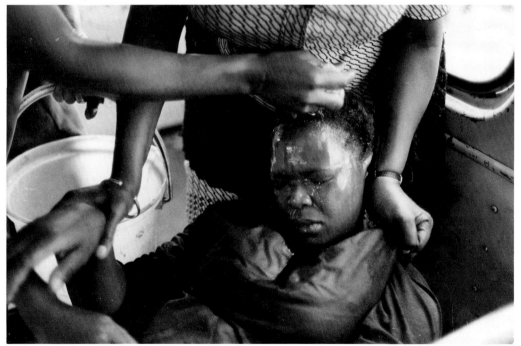

TOP: Throughout the country there were demonstrations in support of the children of Soweto. A large group gathered outside the John Vorster Square police station in Johannesburg; among them were many students and nuns. Defiantly they stood and refused to move. Large numbers of police surrounded them, then they were arrested and taken to the cells.

BOTTOM: This woman was attending the 1978 funeral of a victim of police violence in Soweto when the police attacked the mourners with tear gas. Other mourners revive her.

In June 1976, during the Soweto uprising, because of the unrest in the township, all bus services were suspended by the white-owned bus company, which refused to enter the turbulent township. Dedicated nurses working at Baragwanath Hospital, the largest hospital in the Southern Hemisphere, walked between ten and twenty miles every morning to get to work, then the same distance home each night. They nursed the hundreds of victims who had been shot and injured by the police during the uprising.

Steve Biko died of a brain injury sustained while he was in detention on September 12, 1977. Critically injured during interrogation in prison in Port Elizabeth, he was transported naked in the back of a police van to Pretoria, over a day's journey away. He was found dead on arrival. At the inquest held in the Old Synagogue, Pretoria, the police were found not guilty of causing his death. The finding caused an uproar both within and outside South Africa. Here, his wife, Ntsiki, is seen leaving the inquest.

Winnie Kgware, former president of the Black People's Convention, comes to show solidarity and support during the inquest of Steve Biko, the courageous young leader of the Black Consciousness movement who died while under police custody. In her hand she holds a portrait of Steve Biko.

Helen Suzman, the lone opposition Progressive Party member of Parliament and its only liberal voice for thirteen years, stands outside the Johannesburg City Hall with her husband, Dr. Mosie Suzman. Suzman, a tenacious fighter for human rights, fearlessly represented South Africans of all races who found themselves detained and imprisoned for opposing the government. Black South Africans were at that time not represented in Parliament and their organizations were banned, thus they had no official political voice of their own. For thousands of detainees and political prisoners, she was the only link between them, their families, and the government.

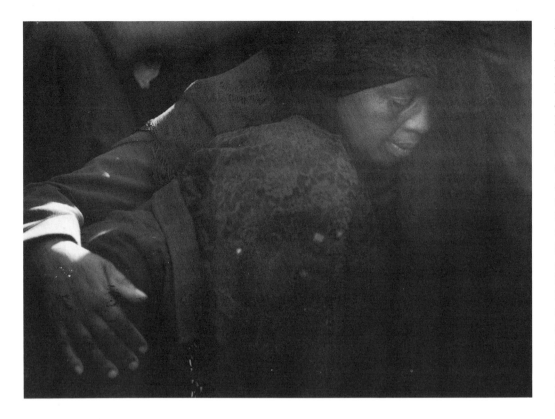

Mrs. Veronica Sobukwe and her daughter Miliswa grieve for their husband and father, Robert Sobukwe. The charismatic leader, an English lecturer at the University of the Witwatersrand, broke away from the ANC in April 1959 and founded the Pan-Africanist Congress. He was instrumental in launching the famous antipass campaign on March 21, 1960, that led to the Sharpeville massacre where thousands of peaceful demonstrators presented themselves for arrest at the Sharpeville Police station because they refused to carry passes. The entire PAC leadership, including Sobukwe, was arrested. Imprisoned, he eventually landed on Robben Island with Nelson Mandela and the defendants of the Rivonia trial. He was released on grounds of ill health and died in Kimberley in 1978.

Anne Pogrund comforts Miliswa Sobukwe on her arrival at Jan Smuts airport from America, where she was studying when she heard of the death of her father, Robert Sobukwe.

In Alexandra township, one of Johannesburg's black ghettos, where ongoing violence is endemic and people are killed daily, streets are barricaded with rolls of barbed wire in an attempt to lessen the violence.

Police brutality toward Wits University students in Jorissen Street, Braamfontein, in 1989.

Colleagues sing "*Hamba Kahle, Qawe*" (Go Well, Warrior) at the funeral of Mrs. Ncaphai, a member of the Federation of South African Women. The federation was active until 1963, when it collapsed because of the arrest and constant harassment of its leaders.

At KwaThema, just
outside the stadium
where a funeral was
being held for the
victims of police
gunfire, a suspected
police informer's car
was overturned by
mourners and set
alight. As the flames
shot heavenward,
these women sang
and danced derisively.

Tokoza is a township to the east of Johannesburg. As in all townships, there are single-sex hostels in which migrant laborers live in large austere dormitories. In August 1990, the male hostel dwellers of Tokoza went on a rampage and attacked the township residents. Many were killed. Since that time,

Tokoza has become a hotbed of unrest, with continuous fighting between the hostel dwellers and the residents. Daily, bodies are found hacked, burned, or shot. This woman's father was murdered by hostel dwellers in February 1991. She weeps as the police remove his mutilated body.

At a funeral in Kagiso township near Krugersdorp on the West Rand, this woman laments for a friend killed when hostel dwellers attacked and slaughtered several people.

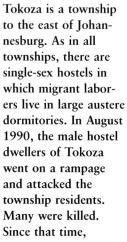

Peter Magubane is
arrested in Alexandra
township while photo-
graphing a march in
1990.

OVERLEAF: The Soweto uprising of June 16,
1976, saw the birth of a new South Africa.
The youth became increasingly militant as
they gave voice to their growing frustration.
They were tired of being oppressed. They
refused to accept passively the injustices of
apartheid as most of their parents had done
before them. It was time for a change. They
rallied together and defied the government.
Here, these girls give vent to their feelings
at the revival of the Federation of South
African Women in 1987.

Walter Sisulu, deputy president of the ANC, and his wife, Albertina. Sisulu, a friend and colleague of Nelson Mandela, was sentenced at the Rivonia trial in 1964 to life imprisonment on Robben Island. He was unconditionally released from prison in 1989 as part of negotiations between the government and the then still imprisoned Nelson Mandela of the ANC. An activist, he was part of the leadership of Umkhonto we Sizwe, the military wing of the ANC. Having been banned, detained, arrested, and imprisoned, he is regarded today as one of the elder statesmen of the ANC. Albertina is equally active. In 1984 she was banned and sentenced to four years of imprisonment for furthering the aims of the ANC but was released pending appeal. Her later appeal was successful. President of the Federation of South African Women, she was also copresident of the United Democratic Front.

Winnie Mandela carries a coffin of a comrade
at a funeral in Emdeni the day before her
husband was released from jail. She was
unaware of his impending release because
the authorities had not yet informed her of
their decision.

TOP: The release of Nelson Mandela, president of the ANC, in February 1990, was welcomed throughout South Africa, and New Year 1991 was a special occasion for him and his family. It was his first free New Year in twenty-seven years. Here Nelson Mandela is seen with his now-estranged wife, Winnie.

BOTTOM: A joyous party was held for Mandela as he celebrated the New Year.

In January 1992, Phola Park township
erupted in violence when rampaging hostel
dwellers attacked the residents. People were
brutally killed, husbands hacked to death in
front of their families, women raped and
murdered, shacks burned to the ground, and
hundreds were left homeless. Mothers fled
the township carrying children on their
backs and their belongings on their heads.
Several bodies were so badly mutilated
they were barely identifiable to shocked
relatives.

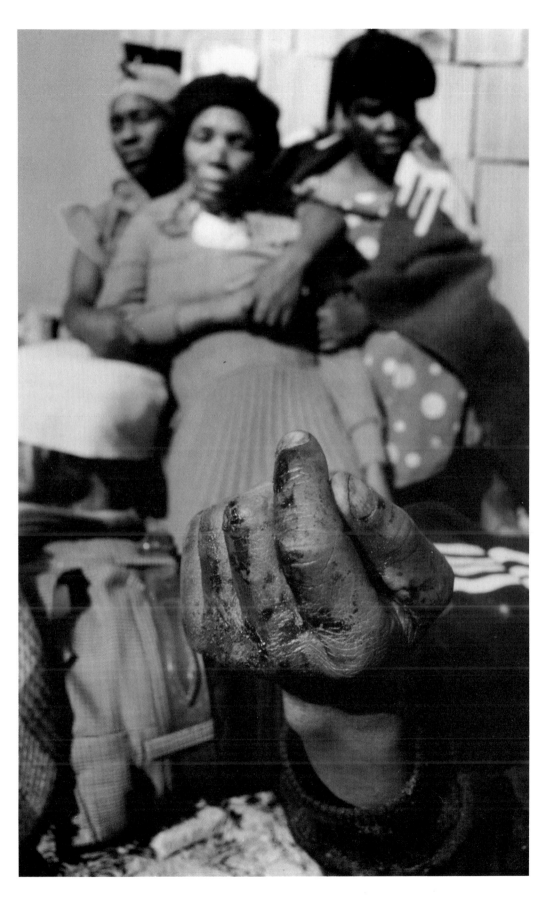

OVERLEAF: The tragedy of the Mamelodi massacre of 1985, where people were shot at by police and a two-year-old child was gunned down in her parents' backyard. The deaths shocked a country that had become almost impervious to horror. A relative mourns for the loss of this baby.

On June 16, 1976, the children of Soweto put themselves in the line of fire to protest apartheid. The power of their unleashed rage in many ways set the winds of change in motion for today's South Africa. Some of these children lived to see the results of their bravery: the unbanning of the ANC, PAC, and AZAPO, the release of Nelson Mandela and other political prisoners, and the abolition of all apartheid laws.

But there is still today much to be done in South Africa. The children of Soweto returned from exile to a country engulfed in violence, where the innocent are murdered, and where the sinister forces of hatred and racism dig in their heels as best they can. I salute the young women and men who put their heads on the block to liberate their minds and the masses from oppression. They are our constant reminder and inspiration of strength, courage, and resistance to evil, and we will not let them down. People of all colors and ages are preparing to walk the last mile. Viva the young lions and lionesses.

— PETER MAGUBANE

*H*elen Joseph died on Christmas Day, December 25, 1992. A valiant and courageous fighter, she dedicated her life to the struggle for a free and just South Africa.

Most of all, we remember Helen as warm and loving, a person of great dignity and modesty, who, in the face of immense personal hardship, was only concerned with the welfare of others.

She was a mother to all.

— PETER MAGUBANE

— CAROL LAZAR

Bibliography

Brookes, Edgar H., and J. B. Macaulay. *Civil Liberty in South Africa* (Oxford University Press, 1958).

Cock, Jacklyn. *Maids and Madams: A Study in the Politics of Exploitation* (Ravan Press, 1980).

Cries of Freedom: Women in Detention in South Africa (CIIR, 1988).

Frederikse, Julie. *The Unbreakable Thread: Non-racialism in South Africa* (Ravan Press, 1990).

The Influence of Violence on Children (Centre for Intergroup Studies, 1990).

Joseph, Helen. *Side by Side* (Zed Books, 1986).

Lipman, Beata. *"We Make Freedom": Women in South Africa* (Pandora Press, 1984).

Pauw, Jacques. *In the Heart of the Whore* (Southern Book Publishers, 1991).

Platzky, Laurine, and Cherryl Walker. *Surplus People: Forced Removals in South Africa* (Ravan Press, 1985).

Reeves, Ambrose. *Shooting at Sharpeville: The Agony of South Africa* (Victor Gollancz, 1960).

Resha, Maggie. *My Life in the Struggle* (Congress of South African Writers, 1992).

Rogers, Mirabel. *The Black Sash* (Rotonews, 1956).

SACHED. *Voices from Young Africa* (Macmillan Boleswa, 1991).

Walker, Cherryl. *Women and Resistance in South Africa* (David Philip/Monthly Review Press, 1991).